Glass and Religion

Glass and Religion

*The Jackson Family and
the First Hundred Years
of the
Tutbury Glassworks*

Philip A. Bell

and

Christopher S. Tipper

British Library Cataloguing in Publication Data.

A catalogue record for this book is available from the British Library.

ISBN 978 0 86071 889 5

A Commissioned Publication Printed by
MOORLEYS
Print, Design & Publishing
info@moorleys.co.uk · www.moorleys.co.uk

This work is dedicated to the memory of our fathers, Wilfred James Bell and Stuart Tipper, both Tutbury-born, life-long Glass Cutters, to the memory of their Glassmaker ancestors, and to our many extended family members for whom the Tutbury Glassworks provided the background to their lives.

Contents

Chapter

1.	Introduction	1
2.	Origins: A Deeply Religious Family	5
3.	A Business in the United States, 1807-1824	17
4.	The Tutbury Glass Works: Beginnings	29
5.	Henry Jackson's Glass Works, 1812-1849	35
6.	The Tutbury Glass Company, 1850-1880	53
7.	William Alexander Sivewright and the FGMFS	63
8.	The Impact of the FGMFS in Tutbury	73
9.	The End of the Jackson Era	81
10.	An Interlude: The Tutbury Flint Glass Co. Ltd	83
11.	Conclusions	93
	Appendix: Benjamin Bell: A Brief Life History	97
	Sources	103
	Acknowledgments	105
	About the Authors	107

Abbreviations

b.	Born
bap.	Baptised
bu.	Buried
d.	Died
CC	Central Committee, FGMFS
CS	Central Secretary, FGMFS
FGMFS	Flint Glass Makers' Friendly Society
FGMM	Flint Glass Makers' Magazine
Jr	Junior
m.	Married
MRC	Modern Records Centre, University of Warwick
Sr	Senior
SRO	Staffordshire Record Office, Stafford
TNA	The National Archives, U.K.
WSL	William Salt Library, Stafford

Cover Illustrations: English Regency Glass, courtesy of Fileman Antiques, Steyning, West Sussex. *Front:* A pair of Regency decanters with step, flute, and diamond cutting, *ca* 1810. *Back:* A set of four elaborately cut Regency decanters and four matching goblets, *ca* 1820. *Frontispiece:* Tutbury Glassworks in the late 1940s.

Chapter 1

Introduction

The Staffordshire village of Tutbury is today a post-industrial commuter community with the only substantial business activity nearby being the Nestlé factory complex across the river Dove in the adjoining village of Hatton, Derbyshire. Its recorded history goes back to the Domesday Book and the Norman Conquest as an estate first of the de Ferrers family and then of the Earls and Dukes of Lancaster.[1] Some evidence of its famous past is visible today; the Priory Church of St. Mary and the remains of its historic castle still dominate the village skyline as they did a hundred years ago and more (Fig. 1). High Street is still home to the half-timbered Dog and Partridge coaching inn and several Georgian houses. But almost all traces of the industries that once supported the village economy and gave work to many—including the glassworks (Frontispiece) and the cotton mill, later a plaster works—have disappeared.

Fig. 1. A view across Tutbury village from the western side of Burton Street, early 1900s. The glassworks is hidden by the field on the left. The castle is on the skyline, centre, with the parish church of St. Mary to the right.

---

[1] Underhill, 1949.

1

The manufacture of lead crystal glassware made an important contribution to the life and economy of the village for two hundred years, from the early nineteenth century until 2012. The enterprises that operated there in the twentieth century—Thomas Webb & Corbett (later, Webb Corbett), Tutbury Crystal, and Georgian Crystal—are familiar names, but surprisingly little information has been available about the origins and early development of this business in Tutbury. How did an industry requiring a highly skilled and specialised labour force develop in a location that was relatively distant from established centres of glassmaking, such as Stourbridge and Birmingham?

Sir Oswald Mosley of Rolleston Hall, in his 'History of the Castle, Priory, and Town of Tutbury in the County of Stafford', published in 1832, recorded that:

> *Works for the cutting of glass vessels were also established at Tutbury twenty-two years ago, the machinery of which is now set in motion by steam, and the manufactory is admirably conducted under the judicious management of Mr. Henry Jackson; the plain glass is made principally at Birmingham, from whence it is forwarded to this place to be cut into patterns and finished. About twenty-two hands are thus engaged.[2]*

Two years later, William White, in the 1834 edition of his History, Gazetteer and Directory of Staffordshire, recorded that Tutbury had '*...a steam-mill, employed in cutting glass, commenced about twenty years ago*'.[3] However, the 1851 edition stated that '*The village has [a] glass works, commenced 1836, and having steam power for glass cutting, etc.*'[4] More recent accounts have provided additional information about the later development of the industry in Tutbury but have added little of substance to Mosley's account of its origins. Thus, the Victoria History of Staffordshire (Vol X, Tutbury and Needwood Forest) records only that:

> *...the continuous history of glassmaking in Tutbury dates from 1810. That year a glass-cutting works was established on the corner of Burton Street and Ludgate Street, probably by a Henry Jackson: it was owned in 1817 and 1820 by Mary Jackson and run by Henry Jackson the younger. By 1832 Henry was using steam powered machinery to cut glass brought from elsewhere,*

---

[2] Mosley 1832, 311.
[3] White 1834, 408.
[4] White 1851, 586.

but by 1839 he was making his own glass, using 40 tons of coal a week in 1840. Henry died probably in 1850 and the works was continued by his widow Eleanor, who in 1851 employed a workforce of 91 men and 9 women. The family traded as the Tutbury Glass Co. until 1880 when the works was closed.[5]

The shortage of facts has probably contributed to the development in recent times of what are clearly myths regarding the Jackson family and their role. Publicity materials and newspaper reports about later Tutbury glassmaking companies contain statements such as the following:

...[the] factory was built in 1836 by Henry Jackson, who bought blanks for cutting. He and his brothers later moved to America.[6]

Encouraged by Henry Jackson, whose brother went to [the] U.S.A. to become the legendary General 'Stonewall' Jackson, glass making developed over the years...[7]

The history of glass making at Tutbury goes back to Roman times and was certainly well established at the time of Henry VIII. The premises...had been run from the early eighteenth century by a remarkable local family called Jackson. Three Jackson brothers emigrated from Tutbury to the U.S.A. and set up glass making in Baltimore. It was a vigorous branch of the family and the Jackson name emerged in a number of prominent personalities including a Bishop, a President of the U.S.A., and the famous Civil War General, 'Stonewall' Jackson.[8]

There is a germ of truth in these statements, but the claim that there was a relationship between the Tutbury Jacksons and Confederate General 'Stonewall' Jackson has absolutely no factual basis. Thomas Jonathan 'Stonewall' Jackson (1824-1863) was American-born with Scots-Irish roots, the great-grandson of John Jackson, a Presbyterian from Coleraine in Northern Ireland who was shipped to America from London in 1749 to serve a seven-year indenture for theft. Nor is there any relationship between the Tutbury family and Andrew Jackson (1767-1845), son of another Scots-Irish immigrant, victor over the British at the Battle of New Orleans (1815) and seventh President of the United States. The claims, of

---

[5] Tringham 2007, 96-97.
[6] *Derby Evening Telegraph,* 2 March 2002, 14.
[7] Company information leaflet, Georgian Crystal (Tutbury) Ltd, no date but ca. 2000.
[8] 'The story of English full lead crystal', Royal Doulton Tableware Ltd., 1976.

course, were probably driven more by marketing concerns than by respect for facts, but they persist. For example, Jason Ellis, in his generally authoritative account of the development of glassmaking in Stourbridge and Dudley, records in a footnote that '*A glassworks was established in Ludgate Street, Tutbury, Staffordshire in 1720 by the Jackson Family (who are reputedly related to General Andrew "Stonewall" Jackson, seventh President of the United States).*'[9] Ellis has not only repeated the myth but has conflated Thomas J. Jackson with Andrew Jackson.

The other component of these myths, the view that there is a continuous history of glassmaking in Tutbury going back to medieval times or earlier, is equally unsubstantiated. It derives firstly from a brief reference to Thomas Wakelyne of Abbots Bromley, 'Glassmaker', being sued for forcible entry in 1472,[10] and secondly from the fact that members of the Henzey family of glass makers, originally from Lorraine, began to make glass (almost certainly window glass) at Bagot's Park near Abbots Bromley, Staffordshire, in 1585. They had been attracted to Sir Richard Bagot's heavily forested estate by the availability of timber for their furnaces, but the undertaking ended when the use of timber for glassmaking was banned by King James I in 1615.[11] Although there may have been unrecorded instances of forest furnaces elsewhere in the Needwood area, there is no evidence whatsoever to link any such enterprises with the later development of glassmaking in Tutbury.

The story of the first hundred years of the Tutbury glassworks is told in the chapters that follow; its later history under the ownership of Thomas Webb & Corbett Ltd and their successors remains to be studied. A wealth of information regarding the Jackson family and their role in the development of glassmaking in Tutbury has been discovered recently, not only from traditional sources such as record offices, archives, and libraries but also from resources available through the internet. Digitised records from England and the United States, including Historical Society archives, genealogical databases, and fully searchable texts of older books, periodicals, and newspapers have revealed that the Jacksons were a deeply religious family, who produced not only a line of glassmakers but also a dynasty of influential clergymen. The reality has turned out to be more complex and more interesting than the myth.

---

[9] Ellis 2002, 375.
[10] Underhill 1949, 127.
[11] Ellis 2002, 46-48.

Chapter 2

Origins: A Deeply Religious Family

The founder of the glassworks at Tutbury was not the Henry Jackson mentioned in the Introduction but his father, William Jackson (Fig. 2). William Jackson was baptised in 1757[12] at St. Mary's Priory Church, Tutbury, the third son of Michael and Susannah Jackson. Michael Jackson's occupation is unknown, but he appears to have been among the more prosperous residents of the village, judging from his appearance in the Land Tax returns as early as 1764.[13]

William Jackson of the parish of Tutbury, bricklayer, married Mary Butler of Kinver parish at Kinver, Staffordshire on 3 April 1780. Kinver is to the west of Stourbridge, about as far from Tutbury as one can get within the county. The parents of bride and groom were not named in parish registers in this period, but other evidence establishes that the bride was the daughter of John Butler and Mary Congreve, who were themselves married at St. Mary's, Lichfield on 2 May 1749. For example, Edward Butler, baptised at Cannock in 1762, was the son of John and Mary Butler. He became a clockmaker in Tutbury and died there in 1833. In his will, Edward left a bequest of *'the clock in my dwelling house at Tutbury'* to Henry Jackson of Tutbury, the son of Mary (Butler) Jackson; he identified Henry as his nephew in his will.[14] Furthermore, several descendants of William and Mary Jackson were given the name Congreve, and some reported that *'On the maternal side they were descended from the Congreves, and very nearly related to Sir William Congreve, the poet. Sir William's inkstand was in the possession of Rev. J. Edward Jackson.'*[15] Rev. J. Edward Jackson was the second son of William Jackson and Mary Butler.

The circumstances that led this 22-year-old native of Tutbury to get married in Kinver are unknown but the proximity of Kinver to Stourbridge

---

[12] A genealogy of the Jackson family is available at Tutbury Museum.
[13] SRO: D3353/9/2.
[14] SRO: Will of Edward Butler, Probate 17 Oct 1833.
[15] Scharf 1881, 774. The author has confused the untitled William Congreve, poet and dramatist (1670-1729), with Lieut.-Gen. Sir William Congreve, 1st Baronet (1742-1814) or his son, Sir William Congreve, 2nd Baronet and rocket artillery pioneer (1772-1828). It is of little consequence, since Mary Butler was related to all three.

is noteworthy; it is possible that the young William Jackson was first exposed to the commercial potential of glassmaking during his time there.

The Principal Actors:

Generation

1   Michael Jackson (1715-96) m. Susannah (1715-90)

2   *Son of Michael & Susannah:*
William Jackson (1757-1812) m. Mary Butler (1755-1822)

3   *Sons of William & Mary:*
Thomas Jackson (1781-1838)
J. Edward Jackson (1783-1845)
Henry Jackson (1787-1849) m. (1) Sophia Chawner (1792-1830); (2) **Eleanor Goolden** (1801-74)
William Jackson Jr (1793-1844)

4   *Children of Henry & Sophia:*
Caroline Jackson (1820-82)
William Henry Jackson (1824-1902)
Mary Ann Jackson (1828-1912)

The Minor Players:

1   Ann Maria Congreve (1732-99): *Aunt of Mary Butler*

2   Henry Jackson Sr (1755-1849): *Brother of William Jackson*
Edward Butler (1762-1833): *Brother of Mary Butler*

Fig. 2. Members of the Jackson family referred to in this account, and their role in the development of the Tutbury Glass Works, 1810-1880. Bold type indicates involvement in the glass business. Henry Jackson Senior, William's brother, plays only a peripheral role in this story; mention of 'Henry' or 'Henry Jackson' always refers to William's son.

William and Mary Jackson settled in Tutbury after their marriage and baptised their first son, Thomas, there on 16 April 1781. The couple had four more children, all boys, over the next twelve years: Johannas Edward (called Edward by his family, bap. 21 April 1783), Henry Jr (bap. 6 May 1787), James (bap. 29 August 1790), and William Jr. (b. 30 January 1793, bap. 4 April 1793). James died in a tragic accident in 1799, but the other children survived to adulthood.

William Jackson and his family were substantial, middle-class members of the Tutbury community. William may perhaps be thought of as a builder rather than as a bricklayer in the modern sense of the term, but he did not remain a bricklayer for long; the Universal British Directory of 1790-93 lists him as a grocer, his brother Henry as a joiner, and his brother-in-law Edward Butler as a clock and watch maker.[16] Edward Butler had arrived in Tutbury at some point in the 1780s; he married Mary Tabberer there in 1789. William, Henry (Senior) and their father appear as property owners in the County Quarter Sessions copies of the Land Tax returns throughout the 1780s and 1790s;[17,18] each held freehold property worth two pounds a year or more and was thus qualified to vote.

Few Land Tax records remain for Tutbury apart from the Quarter Sessions copies, but both the valuations and the assessments for 1795 have survived, albeit as possibly later copies, and they reveal that William Jackson and his family had accumulated significant property holdings by that date.[19] Michael Jackson, by then widowed, resided at a house and garden he owned on Church Street but also owned another house on that street and three in High Street. Those on High Street were subsequently bought (probably on Michael's death) by Charles Bott, one of the partners in the cotton mill, and demolished to make way for his new house. William himself owned and occupied one of the most valuable houses in the village, a house in High Street, but in addition owned six houses and a malt house in Monk Street— property valued in total at fourteen pounds a year. Henry Sr also lived on High Street, in the house immediately adjoining William's; he too owned additional property, a house and garden in Burton Street.

---

[16] WSL: PN4246.

[17] The Land Tax was an annual tax based on the valuation (annual rental value) of land and buildings. The tax was nominally assessed at a rate of four shillings in the pound but seems to have been charged at a much lower rate for Tutbury during the 1700s, perhaps because it was also based on a county quota. The assessment for 1795, for example, appears to represent a rate of approximately one shilling and six pence in the pound (plus a Poor Rate of six pence in the pound). Copies of the tax lists (of limited coverage before the mid-1790s) were made for Quarter Session records, since ownership of freehold property worth two pounds or more a year was a requirement for the right to vote.

[18] SRO: Q/RPL/3/40A.

[19] SRO: D3453/6/13.

William's house, presently known as Granville House, 7 High Street, is reportedly of late 18th century date; it may have been built for or by him.[20]

William's circle of relations in Tutbury also included another of his wife's relatives, her aunt, Ann Maria Congreve. Miss Congreve, a spinster, was the youngest sister of Mary Jackson's mother, and probably had moved to Tutbury in the 1780s to live with William and her niece. By 1792 she too owned property in Tutbury, described in 1795 as five houses in Ludgate Street.

Fig. 3. Jackson family memorials in Tutbury Churchyard. From left: 1, John (d.1788) and Mary (d. 1779), children of Michael & Susannah Jackson; 2, James (d. 1799), son of William & Mary Jackson; 3, Anna Maria Congreve (d. 1798); 4, Michael (d. 1796) & Susannah Jackson (d. 1790). These slate gravestones all appear to be by the same hand and to date from about 1800. They have weathered much better than later memorials of a different stone; Henry and Eleanor Jackson's nearby memorial is only partially legible. Memorials may also exist for Henry's first wife, children Harriet and Sophia, and his parents, but be too weathered to identify.

Michael Jackson died a few days before Christmas 1796, aged 80, and was buried in the churchyard at Tutbury, where his gravestone and those of other members of the family can still be seen today (Fig. 3). They point to a degree of affluence at a time when few had memorials to mark their burial site. His two houses in Church Street subsequently passed into

---

[20] 'Number 7 with house adjoining, List Entry Number 1374394', *The National Heritage List for England,* <https://www.historicengland.org.uk/listing/the-list/>, accessed 29 Mar 2022.

William's ownership, as did Miss Congreve's houses in Ludgate Street after her death in 1799. William also inherited the residue of Miss Congreve's estate, apart from a bequest of fifty pounds to his eldest son, Thomas. Clearly, by the beginning of the nineteenth century, William Jackson had accumulated a substantial amount of property and other assets. However, he does not appear to have been focused on wealth and position so much as on the spiritual well-being of his family and community, for he was a convinced evangelical Christian.

A mid-nineteenth century memoir of one of his grandsons notes that William Jackson was a deeply religious man with evangelical leanings: '*Mr Jackson was a member of the Church of England, ardently attached to her evangelical doctrines, apostolic ministry, and scriptural liturgy. His house was a centre where some of the choicest spirits in the ministry of the Church of England were often gathered.*'[21] Despite their attachment to the Church of England, William Jackson and his sons often described themselves as moderate Calvinists. As members of the 'Low Church' wing of the Church of England, they held views like those of John Wesley and the Methodists but chose to remain within the Established Church.

The memoir includes a sketch of the family contributed by the Reverend Charles Mann, Rector of Abingdon and Ware parishes in the Diocese of Virginia of the Protestant Episcopal Church of the U.S.A. and husband of a granddaughter of William Jackson. The information is third hand at best, prepared some fifty years or more after the events described, and so should be treated as family legends that may have become distorted as they were handed down through the generations. Rev. Mann wrote:

> When his [William Jackson's] children, four sons, were of an age to make the character of the teaching they received in the Church of supreme importance, the church at Tutbury became vacant by the death of the Rector: and under the unfortunate organization of the Church of England, the living was presented to a man for whose religious character and habits of life Mr Jackson could have no respect.[22]

This clearly refers to the death of the then Vicar (not Rector), Henry Babbington, on 22 May 1785. He was succeeded by the Reverend Joseph Clowes, licensed as Vicar of Tutbury on 29 June 1785. Clowes, evidently the clergyman of whom William Jackson disapproved, was an absentee

---

[21] Cummins 1856, 8-9.
[22] Ibid., 9.

priest who lived at Uttoxeter and held several livings in plurality.[23] By 1786 he was Vicar of High Offley as well as Tutbury, and Perpetual Curate of Rocester and of Croxden; he employed curates at Tutbury and elsewhere. Clowes' appointment to Tutbury set in motion events which affected not only the religious life of the Jackson family, but likely also influenced the establishment of the Tutbury Glass Works. The sketch continues:

> *He [Jackson] believed that he was to seek first the kingdom of God for his children; and as the pastoral care the Church had provided did not promise to aid him in this high object, he at once decided, though with deep and heartfelt regret, to seek religious instruction for his family, and especially for his sons, in other folds than that which his heart and judgment preferred. Acting upon this conviction of duty, he built a dissenting chapel, and employed an Independent minister, whom he well knew, stipulating with him, that in the event of the death or removal of the rector of the parish church, and the appointment of a successor of evangelical sentiments, the chapel should be closed, and its preacher seek a congregation elsewhere. Under the ministry of this dissenting preacher, Mr Thomas Jackson, his eldest son, became pious, and soon felt himself called to preach the Gospel. In carrying out this purpose, he went first to a dissenting Theological School, and was licensed to preach among the Independents. Soon after he was licensed to preach, the Rector of Tutbury died, and his successor was such a man as the elder Mr Jackson had desired as his own pastor and the guide of his children. The dissenting minister was then reminded of the agreement made some years before between Mr Jackson and himself, and most honourably avowed his intention of removing from Tutbury...The chapel thus closed was removed and made part of Mr Jackson's manufactory.[24]*

This is a good story which undoubtedly reflects the religious viewpoint of William Jackson with accuracy, but it is by no means certain that it describes the events which took place, nor their timeline, with similar fidelity. However, the early records of the Independent Chapel in Monk Street, Tutbury (now the Ebenezer Congregational Chapel) have survived,

---

[23] 'Joseph Clowes (CCEd Person ID 10080)', *The Clergy of the Church of England Database 1540-1835,* <http://www.theclergydatabase.org.uk>, accessed 29 Mar 2022.
[24] Cummins 1856, 10-11.

and they tell a story with complementary elements.[25] These records contain a brief history of the foundation of this dissenting chapel, written in 1804, in which is noted that:

> *Excepting the occasional labours of the Methodists, we do not know that the Gospel of Xt was ever preached in the place [Tutbury], till an attempt was made about twelve years ago, by the united efforts of the Rev. Mr Smith, then of Derby; & the Rev. Mr Cole, then of Uttoxeter: one or other of whom, preached nearly once a month, for almost four years. However, not meeting with sufficient incouragement [sic], they were obliged to decline their labours.*

Confirmation of the fundamentals of both stories is provided by a document requesting the registration of a Dissenting Meeting House in Tutbury, found in the records of the Staffordshire County Quarter Sessions for Michaelmas 1792. This document reads as follows:

> *We whose names are hereunto subscribed being Protestant Dissenters of the Independent Denomination, do certify, that a Building in Ludgate Street, in the Town of Tutbury and County of Stafford, the Property of Ann Miriah Congreve Spinster and adjoining to the dwelling house of John Forbes Breeches maker and in the possession of Ann Miriah Congreve is set apart as a place of Religious Worship for Protestant Dissenters and request that it be registered among the Records of your Court according to an Act of Parliament made in the first year of the Reign of their late Majesties King William and Queen Mary titled "An Act to exempt their Majesty's Protestant Subjects Dissenting from the Church of England from the Penalties of certain Laws" as Witness our Hands this first Day of October in the year of our Lord One thousand Seven Hundred and Ninety two. (Signed) Willm Jackson; George Smith; John Woodman; Charles Smith; Hannah Rowlinson; Joseph Walkeden.[26]*

So, William Jackson did indeed play a key role in setting up a Dissenting Meeting House, although the property belonged not to him but to his wife's aunt. If the story in the Congregational Church records is taken

---

[25] Independent Chapel, Tutbury: *Records of the Church of Christ assembling in the Independent Chapel, Tutbury, Staffordshire.* Transcript at Tutbury Museum.
[26] SRO: Q/SB 1792 M/115.

into account, it is likely that he would also have been the one to recruit the ministers from Derby and Uttoxeter; he may have paid them an honorarium or expenses, and he may even have arranged that they would leave if a more suitable Vicar was appointed. It seems clear, however, that support was lacking and that the venture failed about 1796. But the memoir's story probably conflates incidents connected with successive attempts to establish a Dissenting Meeting House, for the Congregational Church history continues:

> *After this, a dark cloud seemed again to hang over the place. Nor was it likely to be dispersed, till about the month of June 1799. And then it was that God, whose footsteps are planted in the mighty deep, put it into the hearts of Mr Francis Greasley & Mr William Jackson, both of Tutbury, to fit up a small, but comfortable place, for the regular dispensation of the word of life.*

Francis Greasley, one of the partners in the Tutbury cotton mill, is said to have been persuaded by his wife to convert a barn in Church Lane into this chapel.[27] His role is well known, but William Jackson's involvement has not been noted previously, even though he was one of those petitioning the Bishop of Lichfield for registration of the chapel on 20 September 1799.[28] Although the chapel was opened for worship on 14 November 1799, a congregation or society of ten members was only formally constituted on 23 December 1801. Francis Greasley and his wife were the first two members; William and Mary Jackson were the third and fourth.

Under the ministry of Benjamin Brook, a graduate of Rotherham Independent Academy, the Church Lane chapel thrived. Brook joined the congregation in 1801, presumably as a licensed preacher, and was ordained in the chapel on 18 August 1802. He was a diligent minister and an able ecclesiastical historian, the author of several books. He, rather than anyone connected with the earlier venture, must have been the dissenting preacher under whose ministry Thomas Jackson became pious. Indeed, at a meeting of the members of the chapel on 20 August 1802:

> *Thomas Jackson was proposed to become a Member. His thoughts being directed towards the Xtian Ministry, & wishing to go to the Independent Academy, Rotherham; & the regular time of admitting new Students being near at hand, the Members present*

---

[27] B.B. [Brook, Benjamin] 1820; Matthews 1924, 183-185.
[28] Donaldson 1960, 3.

decreed it expedient to appoint a special meeting, on 27ᵗʰ Inst, on his account.

Rotherham and similar academies were established to provide a university-level education for dissenters and to train their ministers. On 27 August:

According to previous appointment, there was a special meeting of the Church, on Thomas Jackson's account. After reading his experience; & making all necessary inquiries concerning his views of the Gospel, his motives, & conduct, he was unanimously admitted a full Member of Church. This being done, his having the Ministerial work in prospect it was taken into particular consideration; & after minute examination of his knowledge of the things God, his motives, &c; he was unanimously recommended to the Rev. Dr. Williams, Rotherham, as a Student in the Academy under his care.

Clearly, the chapel exerted a significant degree of control over the lives of its members, admitting only those who demonstrated a desire to live a godly life and excluding those who, in the members' view, faltered. So, on 14 October 1803, the records note that:

...though it was exceedingly painful, duty constrained us to examine the conduct of Wm Jackson. When it too evidently appeared, that he had very materially changed his religious sentiments, that he had done much to sew discord among us, & that he had laboured much to injure the cause of Xt: also that, in giving up the accounts belonging the Church, which hitherto he had kept, he had deliberately withheld betwixt thirty & forty pounds of his promised subscription. These things being maturely considered, it was unanimously agreed that he should be no longer a member with us.

The exclusion of William Jackson was quickly followed by the withdrawal of Mary Jackson from the society. This is the point at which the chapel records can be reconciled with the Jackson memoir. As noted above, the memoir records that 'Soon after he [Thomas Jackson] was licensed to preach, the Rector of Tutbury died, and his successor was such a man as the elder Mr Jackson had desired as his own pastor and the guide of his children.' But the absentee Vicar, Joseph Clowes, did not die until

28 April 1812,[29] much later than the timeline suggested by this account—and William Jackson died five days earlier, on 23 April 1812. However, during the early 1800s, Clowes employed as curates at Tutbury two men who would have been much more acceptable to William Jackson. The first was Thomas Cotterill, who was ordained deacon on 19 December 1802 and licensed as curate to Tutbury at a salary of thirty-six pounds per year.[30] He was to become a prominent evangelical churchman, a writer and compiler of hymns and author of a widely read collection of family prayers. Cotterill's appointment, not the death of Clowes, must have been the catalyst that caused William Jackson to change his religious views, be excluded from the dissenting chapel, and rejoin the Church of England.

William Jackson and his family (except for Thomas) soon began to worship again at the parish church. The Rev. Charles Mann's sketch of the family concludes as follows: '*Under the ministry of the new Rector of Tutbury, Henry, Edward and William, the other sons, became pious and attached members of the Church of England; and Edward and William subsequently removed to this country [the U.S.A.] as agents for their father's manufactory.*'[31] They did not enjoy Thomas Cotterill's ministry for long, as he was appointed Perpetual Curate of Lane End (Longton), Staffordshire on 27 September 1805. His successor as curate of Tutbury was the Reverend George Watson Hutchinson, a graduate of Lincoln College, Oxford. A monument to him in Tutbury Priory Church (Fig. 4) records that he was the eldest son of Elisha Hutchinson of Birmingham, and grandson of Thomas Hutchinson, the last colonial governor of Massachusetts. Hutchinson was ordained deacon and appointed curate of Tutbury on 25 January 1806, ordained priest and licensed as curate of Tutbury on 24 May 1807, and appointed Vicar on the death of Joseph Clowes in 1812; he served as a much-loved Vicar until his untimely death of pulmonary consumption (tuberculosis) on 11 May 1818, at the age of 36.[32] It is clear from the memoirs that the Jackson family considered both Cotterill and Hutchinson to be their spiritual mentors.

---

[29] 'Joseph Clowes (CCEd Person ID 10080)', *The Clergy of the Church of England Database 1540-1835,* <http://www.theclergydatabase.org.uk>, accessed 29 Mar 2022.

[30] 'Thomas Cotterill (CCEd Person ID 10150)', *The Clergy of the Church of England Database 1540-1835,* <http://www.theclergydatabase.org.uk>, accessed 29 Mar 2022.

[31] Cummins 1856, 11.

[32] 'George Watson Hutchinson (CCEd Person ID 12620)', *The Clergy of the Church of England Database 1540-1835,* <http://www.theclergydatabase.org.uk>, accessed 29 Mar 2022. Hutchinson's death is erroneously listed as 11 June 1818.

Fig. 4. Memorial tablet to Rev. George Watson Hutchinson, M.A. in Tutbury Priory Church. The tablet is no longer in its original position in the chancel but is now on the North wall of the North aisle.

In 1808, William Jackson and his son Henry became involved in a cause célèbre, the case of Ann Moore the 'Fasting Woman of Tutbury', who claimed to have existed without food or drink since 1807. She lived in one of the Ludgate Street houses that William had inherited from Miss Congreve, a small cottage with one room down and one up. The Jacksons did not believe her story, but one of the few who did was the Rev. Hutchinson, who persuaded William to investigate.[33] She was moved to

---

[33] *Democratic Press (Philadelphia, PA, USA)*, 21 Apr 1809, 2.

the Jackson house in High Street and watched for sixteen days by a large group of local people, organised into 4-hour shifts by Henry Jackson Junior. This failed to detect any fraud, but instead gave her more publicity and profit.[34]

When she began to claim that her ability to fast made her a messenger of God, she came to the attention of Legh Richmond, Rector of Turvey in Bedfordshire and a prominent evangelical churchman. He first visited Tutbury in August of 1810, then came again in 1812 and persuaded Sir Oswald Mosley to organise a committee of clergy, magistrates, and doctors to undertake a thorough examination of Ann Moore's claims.[35] She was watched this time in her own cottage, where fraud was finally detected after she had been watched for nine days.[36]

---

[34] Anon. 1809.
[35] Anon. 1813.
[36] Richmond 1813.

Chapter 3

A Business in the United States
1807-1824

Thomas Jackson, William's eldest son, was beginning his second year at Rotherham Independent Academy at about the time his father was excluded from the Tutbury chapel. He continued with his studies there for another two years, but it seems that he too was becoming increasingly unsympathetic towards Independent Dissent, for he was dismissed from the Academy in 1805 for '*dishonesty, insubordination and spreading disaffection*'.[37] This indictment meant the end of his hope of becoming a nonconformist minister, were he still so inclined, and would also have had a more general impact on his reputation and prospects. In these circumstances, he chose to emigrate to the United States of America, probably in company with his brother Edward.[38] Circumstantial evidence suggests that they both moved there about 1806; there is a record of the arrival in Baltimore, Maryland of a Thomas Jackson in 1806,[39] but insufficient information has survived to precisely identify the individual. It is from this time that a Jackson family connection with the glass trade first appears.

Thomas is reported to have joined the Presbyterian Church on his arrival in the United States, a move that may hint at the reason he was accused of spreading disaffection at Rotherham Academy; English Presbyterians and Independents (Congregationalists) were often at odds during the 18th and early 19th centuries over matters of doctrine, especially that of the Trinity. Perhaps he had failed to keep his opinions on such matters to himself. He returned to England and to Tutbury on at least one occasion before 1810, and again appears to have made no secret of his opinions, for the records of the Independent chapel note that, on 22 February 1810:

---

[37] 'Thomas Jackson (Person i.d. 5897)', *Dissenting Academies Online: Database and Encyclopedia 1660-1860,* <http://dissacad.english.qmul.ac.uk>, accessed 29 Mar 2022.
[38] Jackson M A 1861, 1.
[39] 'Thomas Jackson', *U.S. and Canada, Passenger and Immigration Lists Index, 1500s-1900s,* <http://www.ancestry.com>, accessed 10 Aug 2014.

It was resolved that the name of Thomas Jackson should be erased from the Church-Book. The reasons for this, were, that after living some years at distance from us, & being now removed into America; & though when he has come accasionally (sic) to the town, both before & once since he went abroad, he has conducted himself in a very unchristian like manner, & acted as if he did not belong unto us; & some other improprieties.

Edward Jackson settled in Baltimore, the second busiest port in the United States at that time, while Thomas became a resident of Philadelphia, Pennsylvania (see the map, Fig. 5, for the location of these cities). Edward married Harriet Myers (b. 1792, Baltimore) in Baltimore on 12 January 1809. She was the daughter of Jacob Myers Jr and granddaughter of Jacob Myers Sr, a prominent merchant of German origin; her father ran a china, earthenware, and glass warehouse at 55 Market Street. Edward may have worked for Jacob Jr before striking out on his own as a glass and china merchant, first appearing in the Baltimore City directories in 1810 as a merchant on Albemarle Street in the old town; he subsequently moved west to Market Street (later renamed Baltimore Street) in the more fashionable part of town (Fig. 6). Baltimore was a major port of entry for glass imported from Britain, Ireland, and mainland Europe; the city's role in the glass trade, 1780-1820, has been documented previously.[40]

With Napoleonic Europe off-limits, British glass and pottery manufacturers were already exporting to the newly independent United States, so it is not surprising to find Edward listed (usually as J.E. Jackson) as consignee for shipments of glass and earthenware that passed through the Baltimore Custom House and were reported weekly in the Baltimore Price-Current newspaper. The first recorded shipment, on 13 November 1806, was of 47 crates of earthenware from Liverpool, consigned not to Edward but to Thomas Jackson. This was followed on 30 April 1807 by 24 crates of earthenware plus two hogsheads (a 54-gallon cask) of glass, again from Liverpool, addressed to T. & E. Jackson. Apart from a large consignment of earthenware arriving on 2 July 1807, no further entries for Jackson have been unearthed before 1810, when four separate shipments of glass and one of earthenware arrived in Baltimore, addressed to J.E. Jackson, Thomas Jackson, or some combination of the two names.

---

[40] Lanmon 1969.

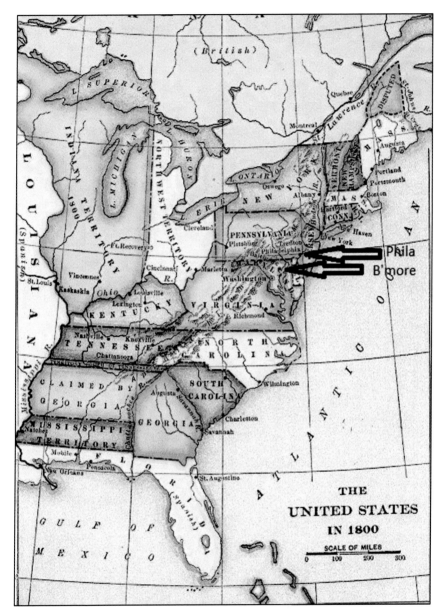

Fig. 5. Map of the United States in 1800. The arrows show the location of Baltimore (B'more) and Philadelphia (Phila).

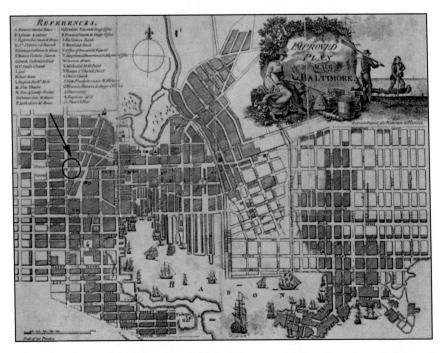

Fig. 6. Plan of Baltimore, 1804. The approximate location of Edward Jackson's Market (Baltimore) Street store is marked with the circle (arrowed). From the Library of Congress, https://www.loc.gov/item/77691636/.

Edward alone is listed as a glass and china merchant in newspaper advertisements and in the Baltimore City directories up to the early 1820s. There are no directory entries in Baltimore for Thomas Jackson, either as businessman or householder, but many entries for him as consignee in the Custom House records until 1823. Consignments to both men consisted only of glass or earthenware; glassware consignments are listed in Table 1 (earthenware consignments have been omitted as irrelevant to this story). The possibility that the Thomas Jackson who is the recipient of these shipments is not Edward's brother, but an entirely different individual, seems unlikely in the absence of any directory entries for another business. Moreover, the entries cover only the period when Edward was in business and cease when he ended his involvement in this trade. In 1817 and 1819, some consignments of glassware addressed to Thomas were shipped from Liverpool to Philadelphia, but that may simply reflect the vagaries of shipping schedules.

20

Table 1: Glassware entered at the Baltimore and Philadelphia Customs Houses, 1807-1823. Reported weekly in the *Baltimore Price-Current* and *Grotjan's Philadelphia Public Sale-Report.* Arrivals are Baltimore except where marked *(P)*, Philadelphia, in the date column. All consignments listed were of glassware only, except for that arriving on 2 Feb 1811, which was a mixed consignment of glass and earthenware. Hhds, hogsheads (54-gallon cask).

Date	Quantity	Consignee	Origin
30 Apr 1807	2 hhds	T. & E. Jackson	Liverpool
10 Mar 1810	8 hhds, 12 crates	Jackson	New York
28 Apr 1810	9 hhds, 31 crates	J. E. Jackson	New York
14 Jul 1810	24 hhds, 5 crates, 2 boxes	Thos. Jackson & Co	Liverpool
3 Nov 1810	5 hhds, 15 crates	M. Jackson	Liverpool
2 Feb 1811	14 hhds, 6 crates, 2 boxes	J. E. Jackson	Liverpool
2 Jan 1813	2 hhds	J. E. Jackson	Philadelphia
9 Nov 1816	5 casks	J. E. Jackson	Philadelphia
23 Nov 1816	36 casks	Thomas Jackson	Liverpool
15 Mar 1817	5 casks	J. E. Jackson	Liverpool
3 May 1817	21 casks, 10 crates	T. Jackson	Liverpool
3 May 1817	60 casks	Thos. Jackson	Liverpool
21 Jul 1817 *(P)*	15 casks, 1 box	Thomas Jackson	Liverpool
6 Sep 1817	14 casks	Thos. Jackson	Liverpool
20 Dec 1817	90 casks	J. E. Jackson	Liverpool
16 May 1818	87 casks	J. E. Jackson	Liverpool
16 Jan 1819	65 casks, 1 case	Thos. Jackson	Liverpool
30 Jan 1819	7 casks, 1 box	Thos. Jackson	Liverpool
19 Apr 1819 *(P)*	85 packages	Thomas Jackson	Liverpool
5 Jun 1819	82 casks	Thomas Jackson	Liverpool
17 Jul 1819	56 packages	Thos. Jackson	Liverpool
31 Jul 1819	35 casks	Thomas Jackson	Liverpool
9 Oct 1819	40 casks	T. Jackson	Liverpool
1 Nov 1819 *(P)*	49 packages	Thomas Jackson	Liverpool
17 Jun 1820	23 casks	Thos. Jackson	Liverpool
16 Mar 1822	5 tierces (casks)	Thos. Jackson	New York
13 Jan 1823	4 casks	J.E. Jackson	Liverpool

More than half of the identified consignments of glassware were shipped to Thomas Jackson, but only 4 of 21 shipments of earthenware were so identified. Edward clearly was the prime mover in the Baltimore business, but Thomas may have had some specific role to play on the glassware side of the business as a partner, or perhaps as a broker, investing his own funds in goods that his brother would then sell. Thomas may have run the business in Edward's absence—in 1816 and 1817, for example, when Edward was in England.

Exactly when Thomas settled in Philadelphia is hard to establish, since there are entries for '*Thomas Jackson, Merchant*' in the Philadelphia directories as early as 1803; these early listings must be for a different person, since the subject Thomas Jackson was at Rotherham Academy until 1805. On 21 April 1809, however, a Philadelphia newspaper reproduced a letter which discussed the case of Ann Moore, the 'Fasting Woman of Tutbury'.[41]

The letter, submitted by Thomas Jackson, was clearly written by William Jackson to a son who was unaware of the story, and so establishes the identity and presence of Thomas Jackson in Philadelphia from about 1807. He certainly arrived no later than 1808, when he married Sarah Goodwin, the daughter of Thomas and Maria Goodwin, in Philadelphia. The couple had two children, William Goodwin Jackson (b. 1809) and Mary Congreve Jackson (b. about 1812).

Thomas Goodwin, Jackson's father-in-law, was said to be an Englishman and is described in directories and advertisements as a merchant, commission merchant or broker. In 1809, he was sharing premises at 298 High Street with Thomas Jackson & Co. The two men were still listed at the High Street address in 1810, but they appear to have gone their separate ways thereafter, and listings for any merchant named Thomas Jackson come to an end following entries in the 1813 and 1814 directories. The nature of Thomas Jackson's business interests in Philadelphia is unclear; he does not seem to have run a store or warehouse, and no business advertisements have been discovered. As suggested earlier, he may have been in partnership with his brother Edward or worked as a broker with his father-in-law.

The War of 1812 may have caused Thomas to search for other means of earning a living, for in March of 1812 an advertisement in a Philadelphia newspaper stated that:

---

[41] *Democratic Press (Philadelphia, PA, USA)*, 21 Apr 1809, 2.

Thomas Jackson, at his Country Residence on the Haverford road, about four miles from Philadelphia, intends opening on the first of April, an institution for a select number of YOUNG LADIES – in which will be taught all the branches of an English education, viz. the English Language, Writing, Arithmetic, Geography, Astronomy, Use of the Maps and Globes, Chronology, Sacred and Profane History, Music, &c &c.[42]

The notice also mentioned that the cost would be 200 dollars per year for all expenses except books. Such an education appears to have had little appeal, however, for the house was for sale only four months later. Although unproven, it seems likely that this individual and our subject are one and the same.

Not long afterwards, Thomas returned to his earlier focus on becoming a minister. He had joined the Presbyterian Church on his arrival in the United States and was ordained as a presbyterian minister in 1814. For the next two and a half years, he was pastor of the Presbyterian Church in Mount Pleasant, New York, but was released from that position in January 1817 when the congregation proved unable to support him.[43] After a visit to England in 1818 he returned to Philadelphia and apparently resumed his working relationship with Edward,[44] although directory listings suggest that he retained his house in Mount Pleasant until 1822.[45] He withdrew from the Presbyterian Church in October 1823, and in 1824 was ordained in the Protestant Episcopal Church.

William Jackson, Jr., the youngest of the brothers, also moved to the United States. When Edward returned to Baltimore in the spring of 1817 after a visit to England, William travelled with him to *'attend to some business transactions of his house'*. After they arrived in Baltimore on 1 May 1817, William spent the next eighteen months travelling on business and assisting Edward,[46] but in the autumn of 1818 he decided to study for the ministry in the U.S.A. He was ordained as an Episcopal priest in 1820.

What brought the brothers to the Baltimore-Philadelphia area and to the glass and china business? Charles Mann believed that *'Edward and*

---

[42] *Poulson's American Daily Advertiser (Philadelphia, PA, USA)*, 5 March 1812, 1.

[43] Alexander 1887, 42-43. The date of Thomas Jackson's installation as pastor is incorrectly given as 2 Aug 1811 (the correct date is 2 Aug 1814).

[44] Jackson M A 1861, 44; 52.

[45] 'Philadelphia Directories', *Books from the Library of the Philadelphia Museum of Art,* <https://archive.org/details/philadelphiamuseumofart>, accessed 29 Mar 2022.

[46] Jackson M A 1861, 35.

William subsequently removed to this country as agents for their father's manufactory'[47] but, as will be seen, the Tutbury glassworks was not begun until about 1810, so Edward (and Thomas) moved there for other reasons. Was it by chance that Thomas settled in Philadelphia and Edward in Baltimore, or were there prior contacts with the Goodwin or Myers families through family, friends, or business acquaintances? Charles Mann's recollections may well reflect the fact that Edward did eventually import glass from the family business and act as its agent. Is it possible that the glassworks came about because Edward or Thomas recognised that additional profits could be made by producing in Tutbury some at least of the glass they were importing into the U.S.A.?

The period around 1809-1810 was not a healthy one for British exporters of glass and china, for relations between the United States and Great Britain were rapidly deteriorating because of British maritime policies and the American response in the form of Jefferson's Embargo Act of 1807. It would have been a difficult time for Edward Jackson, with war with Great Britain looming, so it is not surprising that he decided to demonstrate where his loyalties lay by becoming a U.S. citizen on 28 November 1811.[48] Once war was declared by the United States on 18 June 1812, the brothers would have found it almost impossible to import fresh goods over the course of the next two years as the British blockade of the United States intensified. In fact, except for a small shipment of two hogsheads of glassware shipped from Philadelphia to Baltimore in January 1813, no goods were recorded as being received by the brothers between February 1811 and November 1816.

On the night of 13 September 1814, the British Navy's bombardment of Baltimore's Fort McHenry (coincidentally using Sir William Congreve's rockets) and the sight of the flag still flying 'by the dawn's early light' gave Francis Scott Key the inspiration for the U.S. National Anthem, 'The Star-Spangled Banner'. Edward and his family would have had a grandstand view had they remained in the city. Peace was signed at Ghent on Christmas Eve 1814, and importation of goods from Great Britain began again in 1815. Edward was soon running a successful business from his new shop on Market Street, centre of the shopping district, and importing substantial amounts of cut glass (Fig. 7). Some of

---

[47] Cummins 1856, 11.
[48] 'Johannes Edward Jackson', *U.S. Naturalization Records Indexes, 1794-1995,* <http://www.ancestry.com>, accessed 29 Mar 2022.

this must surely have come from the Tutbury glassworks.

Edward was just one of a number of importers of glass, china, and earthenware in Baltimore during the first quarter of the nineteenth century. No records are known to have survived from Edward's business, but the cash and letter books of one of his competitors, Matthew Smith, still exist in the collections of the Maryland Historical Society. They provide insights into the business practices of these merchants and into the nature of the goods they imported. Smith's business, and doubtless Jackson's too, was both retail and wholesale; his principal customers were dealers from nearby states and further inland. But the merchants also traded with each other; Smith's cash book shows that he and Edward Jackson traded with each other on an occasional basis for small quantities of specific items, probably when needed to complete an order.

ELEGANT CUT GLASS
J E JACKSON
Market st, one door above Liberty st
Has just received per. Brig Panopea from Liverpool, a handsome assortment of Glass, Pitchers, Celery Glasses, Bowls, Tumblers, Wine Glasses, Salt Stands, Hall Lamps, Elec trical Cylinders, Elbows for Electrometers Handles for discharging rods &c.&c. All of which is now opening and will be sold on rea-sonable terms.

Fig. 7. One of Edward Jackson's advertisements, 1817.

The views of Baltimore's harbour and its principal shopping district shown in Figs 8 and 9, although from a slightly later period, nevertheless give some indication of the environment in which Edward built his business. The Baltimore enterprise appears to have been a success up until the early 1820s, when Edward closed his business and became the third of the brothers to enter the ministry of the Protestant Episcopal Church. The final entry in his account with Matthew Smith was made in December 1824, and the account was settled and closed on the first of March 1825.

BALTIMORE FROM FEDERAL HILL.

Fig. 8. 'Baltimore from Federal Hill, 1830'. Print no. 174, engraving, created and painted by William J. Bennett, printed by J.G. Neale at Illman & Pillbrow's, 1831, Cator Collection of Baltimore Views, MS 40, Pratt Library Special Collections Dept. Courtesy Enoch Pratt Free Library, Maryland's State Library Resource Center.

A Business in the United States 1807-1824

Fig. 9. 'Market Street, Baltimore, 1850'. Print no. 168, coloured lithograph, E. Sachse & Co., 1850, Cator Collection of Baltimore Views, MS 40, Pratt Library Special Collections Dept. J.E. Jackson's store would have been in the middle distance, 1810-25. Courtesy Enoch Pratt Free Library, Maryland's State Library Resource Center.

27

Chapter 4

The Tutbury Glassworks: Beginnings

The mid-nineteenth-century American writers of the memoirs discussed earlier clearly believed that William Jackson was the owner (and founder) of the glassworks. He is described[49] as *'the owner of a large and flourishing manufactory'* and his sons Henry and William Jr. were said to have taken over the management of *'an extensive manufactory'* on his death in 1812.[50] But these reminiscences were made at a considerable distance in both space and time. In truth, the glassworks may have had much humbler beginnings. William Jackson is listed not as a glass manufacturer but as a grocer in the Universal British Directory (1790-93)[51] and in an account of the examination in 1808 of Ann Moore, the 'Fasting Woman of Tutbury'.[52] Furthermore, both William and his son Henry identified themselves as grocers in William's will, signed on 19 March 1812, just a month before his death.[53]

Mosley's account of the beginning of the glassworks[54] must be considered authoritative, for he lived locally, was writing of events that happened within his lifetime, and would have been personally acquainted with Henry Jackson, William's son, if not with William himself. In his book, published in 1832, he states that works for cutting glass were established twenty-two years earlier, i.e., about 1810. The founder would have been William Jackson, who probably began the glassworks as a sideline, secondary to his grocery business. The Land Tax returns confirm this, for the 1812 return, but not those for 1809 or earlier, lists 'Glass Shops' in Ludgate Street assessed at two shillings; the assessments for 1810 and 1811 have not survived.[55] The 1812 return lists Mrs Jackson as the owner of the glass shops. It is dated 30 September 1812, some six months after William's death; Mary Jackson would have inherited the business under the terms of William's will.

---

[49] Cummins 1856, 8.
[50] Jackson W M 1847, 16.
[51] WSL: PN4246.
[52] Anon. 1813, 4.
[53] SRO: Will of William Jackson, Probate 13 Oct 1812.
[54] Mosley 1832, 311.
[55] SRO: Q/RPL/3/40B, C.

The works were established on the east side of Ludgate Street and appear to have incorporated the cottages formerly owned by Miss Congreve, including the former meeting house; initially, they may have consisted of little more than these houses. Only one of the cottages inherited by William Jackson remained on the 1812 return, the others having been replaced by the glass shops of similar assessed value. This remaining cottage was occupied by Ann Moore in 1812 and 1813, but it had disappeared from the return by 1814; perhaps the Jacksons had been unwilling to remove her during her period of fame. A later (1843) history of Tutbury clearly states that *'The house she [Ann Moore] occupied in Tutbury now forms a part of the building for the glass works.'*[56] The 1810 Tutbury town map indicates that the works consisted of two parallel ranges of buildings separated by a yard (Fig. 10).[57]

This venture into glass cutting might have resulted from recognition that this, unlike glass making, provided high added value without substantial capital investment or risk. Until the early 1800s, glass-cutting lathes were simple affairs, hand-driven via a large flywheel, worked by women or boys.[58] A small shop with only one or two lathes could be progressively scaled up with relative ease provided the financing was available.

Henry Jackson, the only one of the brothers to remain permanently in England, took over the management of the glassworks at Tutbury after the death of his father, William Jackson Sr, on 23 April 1812; ownership of the business passed to his mother, Mary Jackson, until her death in 1822.[59] Henry is listed in Parson and Bradshaw's Directory for 1818 as a cut glass manufacturer and merchant.[60] He had, no doubt, been involved with the business since its inception and was assisted by his younger brother, William Jr, up to the time of the latter's departure for the United States in the spring of 1817. Although this left Henry in sole control of the management of the glassworks, it does not appear to have been by choice; he had voiced strong opposition to his brother's desire to enter the ministry on the grounds that he needed his valuable aid in the business.[61]

---

[56] Anon. 1843, 73.
[57] SRO: D3453/7/1.
[58] Hajdamach 1991, 39.
[59] SRO: Q/RPL/3/40B, C.
[60] *Parson & Bradshaw's Directory,* 1818, 42.
[61] Jackson M A 1861, 30.

The grocery business must have been closed or sold soon after William Sr's death, for there is no further mention of it after that date.

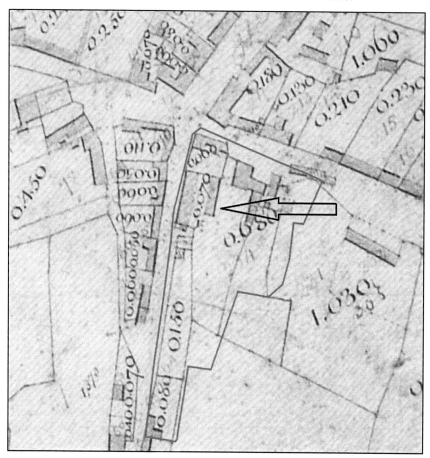

Fig. 10. Part of an 1810 map of Tutbury. The two rectangular buildings presumed to comprise the glassworks at this date are shown by the arrow.

Henry married Sophia Chawner at St. Michael's, Church Broughton, Derbyshire, on 27 May 1819. She was the daughter of William and Sarah Chawner of Lees Hall, Boylestone, only about five miles from Tutbury, and was a descendant of a family that had lived in Boylestone since the late 1600s. Henry and Sophia had five children over the next few years: Caroline (b. 1820), Harriet (b. 1823), William Henry (b. 1824), Sophia (b.

1826) and Mary Ann (b. 1828). Sadly, Henry's wife Sophia died in 1830, leaving him with a family of five young children to look after.

Not surprisingly, he soon remarried; on 4 June 1833 he married Eleanor Goolden at Edgbaston, Warwickshire. Eleanor was born in Moreton on Lugg in Herefordshire in 1801, the daughter of Samuel Eccleston Goolden, 'gentleman'. Her father died when she was five, so she probably had to make her own way in the world, in the manner many young ladies of her social class did, by becoming a teacher. It seems likely that she met Henry Jackson while she and her younger sister Martha were running a small private school for girls in Edgbaston. Martha was running a school on Monument Lane, Edgbaston in 1835.[62] Sophia and Mary Ann Jackson, Henry's younger children, were pupils at the school, then on Vicarage Road, in 1841, and his older girls probably attended the same school in the early 1830s. Two of Henry's daughters died in their youth (Harriet in 1835, aged 12, and Sophia in 1842, aged 15) but the remaining children survived into old age, though neither surviving daughter ever married.

Although he remained a layman, Henry appears to have been as committed to the Church as his brothers. He taught in St. Mary's Sunday School for many years and was a churchwarden in 1829, at the time of the laying of the foundation stone for the new North Aisle; he probably contributed to its cost. A view of Tutbury Priory Church dating from the 1860s is shown in Fig. 11. One of the American memoirs records that he *'was also a successful preacher of the Gospel, by the power of a holy life. In one single year, more than thirty of the workmen in the manufactory made a profession of religion, and avowed that their first convictions had resulted from the example and labours of this devoted servant of God.'*[63] While this statement is very likely exaggerated, it is clear that Henry tried to recruit and retain workers with religious inclinations and reputations for sobriety, and in turn that such men would be attracted by his reputation.

William Henry Jackson, Henry's only son, became the first in the family to go to university; as a prosperous manufacturer, Henry was able to give his son the education he had not received. William Henry Jackson attended Derby School from 1838 to 1843 and then Brasenose College, Oxford, where he gained his B.A. (a third-class degree, a 'gentleman's third' in classics) in 1847.[64] Like his uncles, he went on to enter the

---

[62] *Pigot's Directory,* 1835, 529.
[63] Cummins 1856, 15.
[64] Tacchella 1902, 27.

Anglican ministry, although in his case it was that of the Church of England.[65] Devoted as he was to the church, Henry may have hoped, in vain, that his only son would follow him in the glass trade.

Fig. 11. Tutbury Priory Church from the Southeast, 1860s. The memorial in the left foreground is to John Jackson, a member of another family of Jacksons in Tutbury, whose relationship to Henry's family is unclear. The east end of the new North Aisle, built in 1829 when Henry Jackson was a churchwarden, is visible on the extreme right. A new window at the east end of the nave was also added in 1829. The wall enclosing the east end of the nave would have been built at the dissolution of the monasteries after the central tower and choir had been destroyed. It was not replaced by the present chancel and semi-circular apse until 1868.

[65] *Crockford's Clerical Directory,* 1898, 712.

Chapter 5

Henry Jackson's Glassworks
1812-1849

By the early 1800s, the earlier hand-driven glass-cutting lathes which could produce only shallow cuts in eighteenth-century style were giving way to more powerful ones powered by steam. A trade card of 1807 has survived for W. Wilson, a London firm which supplied 'Steam Mills for Cut Glass' that were capable of making the deep, diamond cuts that the new Regency styles demanded.[66] William White, in his 1834 Directory, noted that Tutbury had '*a steam-mill, employed in cutting glass, commenced about twenty years ago*', i.e., about 1814.[67] On taking over the business, Henry would have recognised that conversion to steam power was necessary for him to remain competitive in terms of styles and productivity. He frequently highlighted this advantage in his advertisements, such as one in the Leicester Journal in 1831 in which he announced a considerable reduction in the price of his glass which '*he is enabled to do, not by manufacturing an inferior article, but...by cutting all his Glass by Steam*'.[68]

Sir Oswald Mosley had noted that, at the time he was writing (1831-32), '*about twenty-two hands are thus engaged*' in cutting and finishing the glass.[69] This is not entirely compatible with the perception in the American memoirs that it was '*a large and flourishing manufactory*'.[70] Flourishing it may have been, but it certainly was not large, particularly at a time when both cutting and polishing were multi-stage processes using the lathe (acid polishing was not used until the 1880s). If the number of hands quoted included all the manual workers—not just cutters and polishers, but also those employed in the boiler house and warehouse—then it was a fairly small-scale operation.

Mosley also stated that the plain glass that Henry Jackson was cutting was made principally in Birmingham. Among potential suppliers, one that

---

[66] Hajdamach 1991, 38.
[67] White 1834, 408.
[68] *Leicester Journal,* 19 Aug 1831, 3.
[69] Mosley 1832, 311.
[70] Cummins 1856, 8.

stands out is the Aston Flint Glass Works, operated by Brueton Gibbins from 1806 and by the partnership of Brueton and William Gibbins from 1812. The Gibbins were Quakers; their works were situated in Aston, Birmingham, adjacent to the Birmingham and Fazeley canal (Fig. 12). Glass loaded onto canal boats at the factory wharf could have been transported safely and quickly (by the standards of the time) to Horninglow basin, four miles from Tutbury, via the Birmingham and Fazeley, Coventry, and Trent and Mersey canals.

View of Aston Flint Glass Works. belonging to Brueton & William Gibbins.

Fig. 12. Aston Flint Glass Works and the Birmingham & Fazeley canal.

The terms of William Jackson's will required that his estate be divided equally between his four sons after the death of his wife,[71] so the fact that the enterprise continued after her death in 1822 suggests that the glass-cutting enterprise had proved sufficiently profitable for Henry to be able to retain the family home and buy out his brothers' share of the business from

---

[71] SRO: Will of William Jackson, Probate 13 Oct 1812.

his portion. The alternative, that Henry's brothers retained a financial interest in the business after 1822, seems unlikely in view of their entry into the low-paid Episcopal ministry; in Edward's case, at least, his inheritance may have facilitated his career change.

Baptisms in Tutbury of glass workers' children reflect the small beginnings and subsequent growth of the operation. The first was that of Letty, the daughter of Susanna and Thomas Pearsall, a glass cutter, at St Mary's church on 15 June 1817 (The new format baptismal registers, introduced in 1813, were the first to record a father's occupation). Interestingly, Mr and Mrs Pearsall gave their abode as Stourbridge; their name is not a local one, and clearly Thomas was amongst those whom Henry Jackson had recruited from the West Midlands to bring the required skills to his Cutting Shop. The steady expansion of the works is mirrored in the increasing number of baptisms of children of glassworkers in the succeeding years:

1817-26	11 children (to six families)
1827-36	20 children (to ten families)
1837-46	66 children (to 20 families)
1847-56	60 children (to 28 families[72]).

The first glassblower, as might be expected, does not appear in St Mary's parish registers until 1837, after the factory's expansion.

No advertisements for glass from the Tutbury works have been found in English newspapers before the early 1820s. Broadsheet newspapers had covered the region for many years (the Derby Mercury, a favoured location for Henry's advertisements in later years, began publication in 1732) and have survived in the archives, so the absence of advertisements is unlikely to be a consequence of the lack of suitable publications or of their survival. It is, of course, possible that Henry Jackson was not free to market his glass as he wished before the death of his mother in 1822. But it is also possible that much of the limited production of the nascent business was exported to Edward Jackson in Baltimore before and after the War of 1812.

The death of William Jackson in 1812, so soon after the enterprise had begun, as well as the outbreak of war, could well have proved a major setback, slowing progress or perhaps even bringing the business to a halt. It would likely have taken the young Henry Jackson some time to assume control of the glass cutting enterprise while dealing with other matters such

---

[72] Including those of great- or great-great-grandparents of both authors.

as the closure of the grocery business. But the arrival of Edward Jackson from the United States in 1816–1817, no doubt with a large shopping list for glass, china, and earthenware, may have been just the stimulus the business needed.

Although documentary evidence is lacking, it is hard to believe that Edward, with a financial stake in the success of the Tutbury glassworks, would not have made every effort to import its products for sale in Baltimore in the years after the end of the War of 1812. But by the early 1820s, the appeal of the American market to Henry may have lessened as Edward prepared to leave the trade and, coincidentally, as domestic American production began to grow. The New England Glass Company, for example, was founded in Cambridge, Massachusetts in 1818 and rapidly became a major producer of many types of plain, moulded and cut glass.

Despite the limited size of the Tutbury factory, advertisements of 1823 and 1826 in the Derby Mercury indicate that Henry had by then built up an extensive business in the East Midlands, with warehouses and/or agents in Derby, Nottingham, Leicester, Lincoln, Boston, and York.[73] He claimed to be able to supply cut and plain glass, to any shape or pattern, of a superior quality, and at reduced prices. The region's nobility and gentry were clearly a key part of his target audience; an invoice has survived from 1824, on Henry's letterhead, billing the Marquis of Hastings for *'72 Flint Rack Glasses'* in three sizes, at ten shillings per dozen (Fig. 13).[74] The Marquis of Hastings, at that time Governor of Malta, owned Donington Hall at Castle Donington near Derby, together with extensive landholdings around Ashby-de-la-Zouch.

Henry's agents also travelled from town to town to sell glass, and occasionally got into trouble for doing so—the Stamford (Lincolnshire) Mercury of 20 April 1821 reported that: '*On Friday the 13th inst. Mr. John Jackson, of Tutbury, in Staffordshire, on the information of Mr. Brocklesby, was convicted before G. Steel, Esq., Mayor of this city, in five separate penalties of £10 each, for selling cut glass without a licence, he not being a resident householder in the city. – The fine was paid.*'[75] This may be the same John Jackson listed in Glover's Derby Directory of 1843 as agent to Tutbury Glass Works, at 5 St. Peter's Street, Derby.[76]

---

[73] *Derby Mercury,* 6 Aug 1823, 3; 19 Jul 1826, 3.
[74] Collection of Tutbury Museum.
[75] *Stamford Mercury,* 20 Apr 1821, 3.
[76] *Glover's Derby Directory,* 1843, 45.

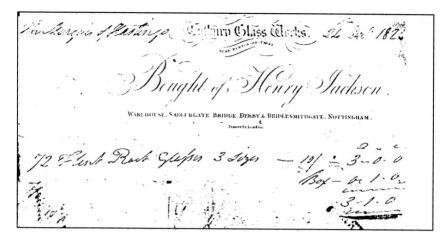

Fig. 13. An invoice from Henry Jackson, 1824. The invoice, dated 24 Dec 1824, is to the Marquis of Hastings for 72 Flint Rack Glasses at 10 shillings per dozen.

Henry was not above hawking his own wares around the country. In an advertisement in the Yorkshire Observer for Saturday 8 March 1823, he announced that he had brought a large assortment of cut glass to the Masonic Hall of the Free Mason's tavern in York, to be sold at wholesale prices.[77] Many of the goods he offered for sale (Fig. 14) are recognisable today; they included decanters, jugs, celery glasses, butters, dessert dishes, tumblers, and wine glasses, as well as less familiar items such as custard glasses and finger cups. An 1834 advertisement by his Derby agent, Joseph Humpston, gives some indication of prices: tumblers from two shillings a dozen, wine and ale glasses from four shillings, and goblets from five shillings a dozen (Fig. 15). For a dozen wine glasses, this is equivalent to £19.65 in 2020 in relation to the retail price index or as much as £180.80 relative to average earnings.[78]

Matthew Smith's Baltimore letter books,[79] mentioned in Chapter 3, also provide insights into the wares being produced by English glass manufacturers during the first quarter of the nineteenth century (the Regency period) that supplement the information in standard works on the

[77] *Yorkshire Observer,* 8 Mar 1823, 152.

[78] 'Five ways to compute the relative value of a UK pound amount, 1270 to present', *Measuring Worth,* <http://www.measuringworth.com/ukcompare/>, accessed 29 Mar 2022.

[79] 'Matthew Smith letter books, 1803-1862', *Smith-Tyson collection: [Matthew Smith Letterbooks 1803-1862], microfilm MS 981.* Baltimore, MD: Maryland Historical Society.

subject. For much of the period, Smith, a neighbour and competitor of Edward Jackson, imported his cut and plain flint glass from William Wilson and Company of Newcastle-on-Tyne. The wares and patterns are likely to be similar to those adopted by Henry Jackson in Tutbury.

Elegant Cut Glass.

To be SOLD at the WHOLESALE PRICES, in the Masonic Hall of the Free Mason's Tavern, Little Blake-Street, York.

H. JACKSON,
Cut Glass Manufacturer,

Respectfully informs the Inhabitants of this City and its Vicinity, that he has brought direct from his Manufactory, at TUTBURY, in STAFFORDSHIRE, to to the above situation,

A LARGE AND SPLENDID ASSORTMENT OF

CUT GLASS,

Consisting of Decanters, Jugs, Celery Glasses, Butters, Desert Dishes, Tumblers, Wine Glasses, Custard Glasses, Finger Cups, &c., and every Article in the above Line, for READY MONEY ONLY.

J. H. trusts, that as the above GOODS are of a superior Quality, and will be Sold at the Wholesale Prices, they will merit the attention of the Public. The Wholesale Price is affixed to each Pattern, from which no deviation will be made. An inspection is respectfully solicited, as the Goods are now open for that purpose.

. Monday next will be the First Day of Exhibition and Sale, and as H. JACKSON'S stay in York is limited, such Ladies and Gentlemen as wish to be provided with CUT GLASS of a quality rarely to be met with, may consider it adviseable to honour the Exhibition with a Visit as soon as they can make it convenient to themselves.

Licensed Hawker, No. 693. A.

March 8th. 1823.

Fig. 14. One of Henry Jackson's advertisements, 1823.

On 18 August 1806, Smith sent a large order to Wilson & Co. via his Liverpool agent for delivery the following spring. Besides a substantial amount of plain glass, the order included some 120 dozen 'French' (defined as 'taper shape') wine, claret, and liqueur glasses, all with fluted stems. Decanters included 2 dozen quart decanters, with 'three rings, cut, fluted and engraved in four patterns' – Navy, Sun, Cornwallis, and Vandyke Borders. Dishes (5-10 inches, round and oval) were ordered cut in patterns described as Pine Apple *(sic)*, Diamonds & Festoons, Husk & Stars, and Festoon & Stars. An order sent to the same company on 13 June 1817 was for a similar assortment of goods, but this time no pattern names were assigned to the wine glasses. Decanters, listed as 'Rodney' decanters, were to be 'fingerd & fluted' or with 'cut rings & fluted', with concave or mushroom stoppers. Cut dishes and bowls were ordered in Husk, Festoon & Stars, and Sun patterns, with bowls also in the Curtain pattern. Many of these pattern names seem, at least in part, self-descriptive.

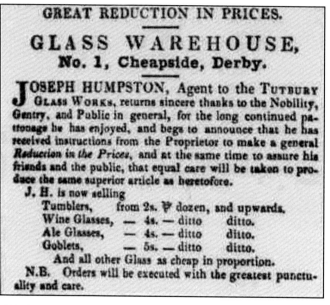

Fig. 15. An advertisement in the Derby Mercury, 17 Sep 1834.

Nineteenth-century glassmakers, unlike their potter counterparts, rarely marked their wares, so attribution of glass to a specific factory is often subjective and depends on the context in which it is found. Thus, a group of glassware with good provenance linking it to Henry Jackson's works was reported recently,[80] consisting of four small open salts and a sugar

---

[80] Personal communication, Henry Moss-Blundell to CST, 2020.

bowl. Family records state that they were purchased during a visit to the Tutbury Glass Works in the summer of 1835 by 15-year-old Mary Elizabeth Ellen Jackson, said to be a second cousin to Henry. She was staying with relatives in Doveridge, Derbyshire at the time and bought the glass as a present for her mother. Her family were originally from Scropton, Derbyshire, a parish just across the River Dove from Tutbury, but during the eighteenth century they had moved to London, where they were cheesemongers. Although the absence of key parish records makes it hard to prove, it is likely that she was descended from a brother of Michael Jackson, Henry's grandfather, and was indeed Henry's second cousin, but twice removed.

Henry was still buying in his plain glass as late as the 1830s; he was not included in the list of glass makers paying the Glass Excise Duty in 1831.[81] This tax, in force until 1845, imposed a heavy administrative burden on glass makers, as well as a financial one, and he would have been anxious to avoid it for as long as possible. But in 1836 he rebuilt and extended the glassworks to include all the facilities necessary to make glass as well as cut it. A plaque with the initials 'H.I' (possibly a misreading, but more likely the latinised initials for Henry Jackson) and the date '1836' was preserved after a later rebuilding in 1952.[82]

The 1840 Tithe Apportionment for Tutbury records that Henry was the owner and occupier of a glass house, blowing house, warehouse, other buildings, and yards in Ludgate Street.[83] Opposite the main works, he also owned and occupied stables, wagon sheds and a yard, approximately on the site of the car park of the present-day Vine Inn. The accompanying Tithe map (Fig. 16) reveals that the new construction included a circular building, unquestionably a glasshouse cone, which would have contained the furnace and glassblowing shop.[84] The furnace and the steam engine consumed a substantial amount of fuel; by 1840, Henry was using 40 tons of coal a week, 20 tons from Swadlincote, and 20 from the Derby Wharf.[85]

---

[81] Hajdamach, 413-415.
[82] Hewitson 2005, 9.
[83] TNA: IR 29/32/217. Digital version:
<http://freepages.genealogy.rootsweb.ancestry.com/~laetoli/tutburytitheapportionment.html>, accessed 29 Mar 2022.
[84] TNA: IR 30/32/217. Digital version: <http://freepages.genealogy.rootsweb.ancestry.com/~laetoli/ tutburytithedetail.jpg>, accessed 29 Mar 2022.
[85] SRO: D603/N/6/13.

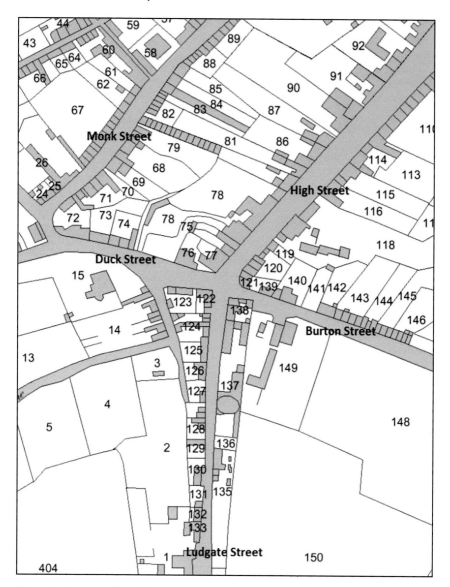

Fig. 16. Part of the 1841 Tithe map for Tutbury. Henry Jackson Jr owned lot 81, his own house and garden; lot 82, houses; lot 129, stables, etc.; lot 133, houses; lot 137, the glassworks. Henry Sr owned his house, lot 80 (between lots 78 and 81), and lot 138, houses.

43

Interior View of Aston Flint Glass Works, belonging to Brueton & William Gibbins.

Fig. 17. Interior of a traditional type of glasshouse cone, about 1820.

The traditional type of English glass cone was designed to maximise the draught and increase the heat supplied to the single, central coal-fired furnace (Fig. 17), but in the early nineteenth century there was a move towards constructing glasshouses with two or more furnaces connected to a chimney. Some of these new glasshouses were built as truncated cones with a large central chimney, others as conventional rectangular buildings.[86] A photograph (Fig. 18), probably taken in the 1870s or 1880s from the fields to the east of the glassworks, shows that Henry Jackson's 1836 glasshouse cone was built in the traditional bottle-shaped style. The chimney to the left of the cone is that of a second furnace, installed in the late 1860s.

---

[86] Hajdamach 1991, 21-22.

Fig. 18. Henry Jackson's 1836 glass cone, view from the south, 1870s or 1880s.

The original cone was rebuilt in truncated form with a central chimney at a later date, as can be seen in a distant view of the Tutbury works from across the village, and in a remarkably atmospheric photograph of Ludgate Street, both dating from about 1910-1920 (Figs. 19, 20). The cone is impressive even in truncated form; it would have dominated the neighbourhood as originally built.

The *Penny Magazine* of 1841 contains an account of a day spent at Apsley Pellatt's Falcon Glass Works in Blackfriars, London. It provides a comprehensive view of the processes used in a glassworks making cut glass during the second quarter of the nineteenth century that are likely to be similar to those used in Henry's new works.[87]

The early steam-powered glass-cutting lathes were usually driven from floor-mounted rollers, with glass being cut either overhand (by a seated workman) or underhand (by one standing).[88] It is likely that Henry also rebuilt his cutting shop in 1836, to the then standard format of two parallel rows of overhand cutting 'frames' for seated workmen, facing each other and driven by leather belts from a central overhead shaft. This shop,

---

[87] Anon. 1841. 'A day at a flint-glass factory.' *The Penny Magazine* X, 81-88.
[88] Hajdamach 1991, 55-60.

fronting Ludgate Street, can be seen in a postcard dating from 1913 (Fig. 21); it survived largely unchanged until the rebuilding of 1952 (Fig. 22). The adjacent cottages on Ludgate Street may have been constructed about the same time as the cutting shop by Henry Jackson Sr. These and the cottages facing Burton Street, also owned by Henry Sr by 1840, were not demolished until Thomas Webb & Corbett Ltd. built a new office block on their site in 1934. An aerial photograph of the glassworks (Fig. 23), probably dating from the later 1940s, shows the new office block adjacent to Henry Jackson's cutting shop and the truncated glasshouse cone (which by this date had lost its chimney).

Fig. 19. View of Tutbury glassworks from the castle, about 1910-1920.
The works now includes a truncated cone with central chimney.

Glassblowers had to be recruited from elsewhere to staff Henry's new blowing shop, and at this time he attempted to recruit religiously inclined workers. An advertisement in the Birmingham Gazette on 7 March 1836 read as follows:

TO GLASS-BLOWERS. Wanted, a complete Set of Workmen in the above business, including Servitors and Foot Blowers, also a Person who has had considerable experience in Metal-making; one who can undertake to superintend the Glass House generally would be preferred. It is particularly requested that none will apply but sober steady men of good character. Serious professors of religion would find this a comfortable place, it having long been the plan with the Proprietor of these Works to conduct them on Christian principles.[89]

Fig. 20. The glassworks, looking south along Ludgate Street, about 1910-1920. This view shows the truncated glasshouse cone and ancillary buildings, including the chimney of a presumed second glasshouse and furnace behind the cone, and that indispensable adjunct to a glasshouse, a public house— the Vine Inn.

---

[89] *Aris's Birmingham Gazette,* 7 Mar 1836, 1.

This approach does not appear to have been merely a means of attracting more reliable workers but rather a practical expression of his beliefs; in like manner, in 1842, he eliminated (or at least minimised) Sunday working in the glassworks.[90]

Fig. 21. Ludgate Street, showing Henry Jackson's rebuilt cutting shop, about 1913. The cutting shop is on the left, beyond the corner cottage and the two that follow.

Henry had completed his rebuilding by 1839, at which time he placed an advertisement in a Leicester newspaper to inform the locals that '*...he has now completed his extensive Glass Houses and Steam Power for the Cutting Department, which will enable him to make a further reduction in his former very low prices'*. He offered a 10% discount for cash on purchases of less than five pounds, and 20% above that sum. He claimed that '*Parties commencing housekeeping...will find his prices of superior Cut and Plain Glass below any retail establishment in the kingdom.'*[91] Henry appears to have made a habit of price cutting, to the extent of undercutting other makers' prices; in 1842, during a period of deep depression in the industry, Benjamin Richardson of the Wordsley Glassworks complained that '*Jackson is the curse of the trade'.*[92]

---

[90] Jackson M A 1861, 274.
[91] *Leicester Journal,* 2 Aug 1839, 2.
[92] Ellis 2002, 347.

Fig. 22. The cutting shop, about 1950. Although built in 1836, the internal layout was essentially unchanged more than a hundred years later.

Expansion of the glassworks resulted in a substantial increase in employee numbers. The 1841 census returns for Tutbury suggest that there were at least 48 employees (all male) at that time; the majority were aged 20-39, with only five being over 40. Of the twenty-one men identified as glass blowers or glass makers (the terms were used interchangeably), seventeen were born outside the county of Stafford (five in Scotland), demonstrating that Henry had recruited experienced workers from elsewhere to support his expansion into glassmaking. In contrast, two-thirds of the twenty-five cutters were born in Staffordshire. No boys under 15 are listed, though some no doubt did work as 'takers-in' in the blowing shop (see Chapter 6). Four excise officers were also living in the village, probably there to assess the Glass Excise Duty; they had left by 1851.

The expansion appears to have been made primarily to enable Henry to have control of his own supply of plain glass, for there is no hint from the 1841 census returns that he was using any skills beyond those of his glass blowers, makers, and cutters. During the 1840s, however, he continued to increase the size of his workforce and, probably after the Glass Excise Duty was abolished in 1845, began to make use of additional technologies for producing or decorating glass. Although the evidence for this comes largely from the 1851 census, the developments apparent at that time must have been put in place over several years. By 1851 the workforce (reported to be one hundred in number) included women, some of whom were employed as roughers, who undertook the first step in cutting (two of whom specifically identified themselves as lamp roughers), and others as glass frosters, responsible for decorating glass in a style then much in demand. Henry may also have experimented with pressed glass, since William Leicester, son of a Warrington glass maker recruited in the 1840s, was listed as a glass presser in the 1851 census.

Henry had become a typical wealthy Victorian entrepreneur by the 1840s. When his younger brother, William, and his wife visited England in 1836, Henry and Eleanor were able to take them on a lengthy tour (presumably by carriage) of the South of England that included London, Kent, Windsor, Oxford, Bath, Bristol, and the Wye Valley.[93] Henry had invested in the Derby and Derbyshire Bank as early as 1835[94] and when 'Railway Mania' struck the English middle classes in 1845, he subscribed for 150 shares of £25 each in the proposed Derby and Crewe Junction Railway and became a member of the provisional committee of the company.[95] Although he only had to pay a deposit of £1-10s.-0d. per share, his total potential investment of £3750 would be equivalent to somewhere between £379,000 and £4.4 million in 2020 terms, depending on the measure for comparison.[96] This proposed railway was subsequently absorbed into a scheme proposed by the North Staffordshire Railway; whether Henry transferred his investment to that company or not is unknown.

Although a London address is listed on his headed notepaper as early as 1824 (Fig. 13), it is not until the 1840s that there is clear evidence that he had expanded his business beyond the East Midlands and part of Yorkshire and was competing in the London market. He had a London agent, Edward Cave, as early as 1842,[97] but towards the end of the decade

---

[93] Jackson M A 1861, 197-208.
[94] *Staffordshire Advertiser,* 4 Apr 1835, 2.
[95] *Derby Mercury,* 21 May 1845, 1; 'Henry Jackson', *Railway Subscription Contracts deposited in the Private Bill Office, 1846.* Parliamentary Papers, House of Commons, 1846, 38(14), 155.
[96] 'Five ways to compute the relative value of a UK pound amount, 1270 to present', *Measuring Worth,* <http://www.measuringworth.com/ukcompare/>, accessed 29 Mar 2022.
[97] *Robson's London Directory,* 1842, 1206.

a Tutbury-born glass cutter named Edward Everton had become his London agent, with a business address in Holborn.[98] Any plans Henry Jackson may have had for the future were to be cut short, however, for he died on 4 October 1849 at the age of 62.

Fig. 23. Aerial photograph of the glassworks, probably from the later 1940s. The cottages on the Burton Street frontage have been replaced by an office block, adjacent to Henry Jackson's 1836 cutting shop, and the truncated cone has lost its chimney.

Henry Jackson was buried at his beloved parish church, the Priory Church of St. Mary, Tutbury, on 9 October 1849; his gravestone still stands alongside those of other family members (Fig. 24). It is not particularly impressive and has been badly eroded by weather to the point that it is barely readable. But there is no memorial tablet of any description inside the church that Henry did so much to support. However, in surprising contrast, inside the church there is a dignified marble wall tablet to the

[98] *Post Office London Directory, Small Edition,* 1852, 1035.

memory of Anne Croft, the twice-widowed mother of Eleanor Jackson, as well as a gravestone in the churchyard—all this in memory of a woman who lived in Tutbury for no more than four years before she died in 1845. Perhaps, for Eleanor, blood was thicker than marriage.

Fig. 24. Henry Jackson's badly eroded gravestone in St. Mary's churchyard, Tutbury.

Chapter 6

The Tutbury Glass Company
1850-1880

In his will, signed on 26 August 1846 and witnessed by his clerks, James Elton and John Barnes, Henry Jackson nominated Eleanor Jackson and William Henry Jackson, his wife and son, as his executors and trustees, and he gave them authority to continue his business for as long as they should see fit.[99] So the business continued, now constituted as a partnership trading under the name of the Tutbury Glass Company. A year after his death, an advertisement in the Derby Mercury on 4 September 1850 noted that:

> *The Tutbury Glass Company (Late H. Jackson), Grateful for past patronage beg respectfully to inform the Inhabitants of Derby and its Vicinity that they still carry on their glass business at their Old Established Warehouse, 17, Victoria Street, where they have made arrangements for keeping a Larger Stock, and thus presenting a greater variety in Plain, Pressed, Cut and Ornamental Glass.[100]*

Henry's widow and daughters remained in the family home on High Street but made some changes. Just three months before Henry's own death, his uncle, Henry Sr, had also died. Henry Sr bequeathed his High Street property to his nephew, Henry Jr, along with two acres of land in Hatton called the Church Land.[101] The younger Henry would have had no opportunity to take advantage of this bequest, but his widow combined the High Street land holdings and altered or rebuilt Henry Sr's house to create an extension of her home; it remains in this form today (Fig. 25).

Eleanor and her daughters, Caroline and Mary Ann, became partners in the Tutbury Glass Company, but it appears that William Henry Jackson, Henry's son, was never involved—was 'trade' beneath this Oxford-educated clergyman? Eleanor also involved two young men from her side of the family in the business in the early years after the death of her

---

[99] TNA: PROB 11/2113/145.
[100] *Derby Mercury,* 4 Sep 1850, 2.
[101] SRO: Will of Henry Jackson Sr, Probate 29 Aug 1849.

husband—perhaps not the wisest decision, since there is no evidence that they had any experience of the glass trade. The first was Frederick Sheldon, a son of Eleanor's elder sister, Mary Ann Goolden. In 1851 this 24-year-old was living with his widowed mother and siblings on Burton Street, Tutbury and was described on the census as a Glass Manufacturer, but he had disappeared from the scene by 1861. White's Directory for 1851 instead lists David Barnes as manager of the Tutbury Glass Company and Sheldon as foreman.[102] The census record, however, gives Barnes' occupation as glass warehouseman. He may have been an interim manager, in place from the time of Henry's death until supplanted by Sheldon a short time before the census. David Barnes was born in Warrington about 1791 and had worked as a glass cutter for Henry Jackson for many years. John Barnes, his son, was born in Tutbury in 1825 and was one of the clerks who witnessed Henry Jackson's will in 1846; by 1851 he was a traveller for the company.

Fig. 25. 7 High Street, Tutbury, home of William Jackson and Henry Jackson Jr. The left-hand part was originally the home of Henry Jackson Sr.

---

[102] White 1851, 590.

The second relative to enter the business was Thomas Eagles Small. He was a stepson of Eleanor's younger sister, Martha Phipps Goolden. She married Thomas Small, a wealthy Birmingham businessman (a manufacturer of 'japanned' ware, i.e. black lacquered and decorated goods) and widower with five children, in 1846 at Tutbury. Martha Goolden and Thomas Small had been near neighbours in Edgbaston in 1841 at the time she was running a private school there (see Chapter 4). By 1851, Thomas and Martha Small and their family (including Thomas Jr) were living at Bladon Castle, Newton Solney, near Burton-on-Trent. Aged 21 in 1851, Thomas Eagles Small was listed as a cut-glass-manufacturer's clerk. But at some point he also became a partner in the company, most probably because he or his father invested capital in the business. This partnership did not last long, for in 1855 an announcement appeared in the London Gazette giving notice that the partnership between the three Jackson women and Small had been dissolved by mutual consent on 30 December 1854 '*so far as regards the said Thomas Eagles Small*'.[103] This may not have been the end of the relationship, however, for Small is listed on the 1861 census as a glass agent living in London. He died in London in 1867.

On the 1851 census, Eleanor Jackson reported that she employed 91 men and 9 women. Only 82 employees can be unambiguously identified from the occupations they reported on the census, however, and 15 of these (six more than identified by Eleanor) were women, including six roughers and six frosters. There were 27 cutters (including roughers) and a combined total of 33 glass blowers and makers; the latter terms were used interchangeably. Only four of the 27 cutters were not born locally, but 15 of the 33 blowers/makers were born elsewhere, including all but one of those aged 30 or above. Clearly, the experienced glass makers from Birmingham, Warrington and other places were by this time training younger local men in their trade. The only white-collar workers identified were Frederick Sheldon, manufacturer, Thomas Small, clerk, John Barnes, traveller, James Elton, agent, and Edward Everton, London agent.

In the glassblowing process, the workers were organised into teams or 'chairs' of four: the workman or 'gaffer', who worked from the glass maker's chair; the servitor, the primary assistant who gathered the glass onto a blowpipe and did the initial blowing; the footman, the second assistant, who provided the additional gather for the feet of wine glasses

---

[103] *London Gazette,* 20 Mar 1855, 1153.

and generally assisted the others; and the taker-in, usually a boy, who carried the finished articles to the lehr (annealing oven) where they were slowly cooled. Apprentices entered the trade as footmen and served a seven-year apprenticeship, normally from the age of fourteen (and after several years as a taker-in). Glass makers worked around the clock, each team working two 6-hour split shifts in a 24-hour period, generally from Monday morning to Friday evening. Thus, there probably were four chairs working each shift, to account for 33 glass makers; the number includes eight boys aged ten to sixteen who were probably takers-in, and therefore reflects the full complement of four workers per chair. Since there were usually two pots of molten glass in the furnace per chair, the works was probably operating an eight-pot furnace at that time.

The Children's Employment Commission reported specifically on the Tutbury factory after an inspection visit in 1865.[104] Mr J. Jones, manager, was quoted:

> *Our principal manufacture is cut glass. The only department in which children are employed is the blowing department. In the blowing house the hands change every six hours. One set work from 7 a.m. to 1 p.m. and then from 7 p.m. to 1 a.m. The change of hands takes place regularly. There are always two sets going. On Monday work begins at 7. They seldom work after 1 o'clock p.m. on Friday.*

The Commissioners spoke to young Thomas Watson in the Blowing House:

> *I am twelve years old. I take in. I have worked a year and a half. I took in when I first came. I came at 1 o'clock last night and worked to 7 this morning and then came again at 1 o'clock this afternoon. On Friday I usually stop at 7 o'clock on Friday night. I don't work on Saturday. I can read and write.*

Thomas Meer told them '*I am 11 years old. I have worked two months. Before I came I worked in the cotton mill. I was a half-timer then.*' And his cousin Herbert Meer: '*I am going twelve. I have worked here more than a year. I can't read. I get 1s a day. I take in.*' All three were sons of glass makers.

It is almost impossible for the modern reader to comprehend the impact

---

[104] Children's Employment Commission 1862, Fourth report of the commissioners, House of Commons Parliamentary Papers, [3548] HC1865, xx, 103. SRO: MF22.

of this alternating six-hour shift system on the lives and health of these children, staggering day and night between the furnace house and their beds in the Ludgate Street and Burton Street cottages a few yards away. Karl Marx suggested that: '*Meanwhile, late by night perhaps, self-denying Mr. Glass-Capital, primed with port-wine, reels out of his club homeward, droning out idiotically, "Britons never, never shall be slaves"!*'[105] How far this characterisation applied to Henry Jackson, or even to Eleanor Jackson and her daughters, is unclear.

Conditions were more normal in the rest of the factory. According to Mr. Jones:

> *In the cutting shop, boys are employed at about 14 years of age. They are taken as apprentices. All are bound by deed for seven years. In the roughing room a few young women are employed. In the grinding and roughing shops the hours of work are from 6 a.m. to half past 6 p.m. On Saturdays they leave off at 2 o'clock in the summer. In the winter they work from half past 6 to 7. They have half an hour for breakfast, an hour for dinner and half an hour for tea. There is never any overtime in the roughing shop. The cutters work overtime sometimes. They never work more than 9 hours at a time.*

But still, over sixty hours a week! Amongst the youngsters quoted was Julia Barker in the Roughing Shop: "*I am 18. I have not worked eight months. Before I come here I was home. I come at 6 o'clock; I leave at 4. In winter I worked to 7 o'clock. I began at half past 6 in the morning. I never get any grit in my mouth. I am paid by the quantity of work I do.*' Charles Vaughan was an apprentice glass cutter in the Grinding Shop:

> *I have been apprenticed two years and four months. Before I was apprenticed I went to school. I can read and write. I come at half past 6 and leave at 7 o'clock in the evening. I have worked to 9. I never worked three days running to 9. I often work to a quarter before 8. That is overtime. We have to work this week to a quarter to 8. I get 4s a week regular wage and may earn what I can over that.*

From Henry Jackson's death until the early 1860s, the small group of long-term managerial employees of the glassworks rotated through the various senior positions. James Elton, first a clerk and then agent, had

---

[105] Marx 1887, 199 (note 71 to Chapter 10).

become manager of the Tutbury Glass Company by 1859[106] (employing 59 men, 16 boys and 10 women in 1861). John Barnes, formerly traveller, had become clerk, and Thomas Small (if, indeed, he was still working for the company) had switched from clerk to agent. The only newcomer to the group was William Sivewright, son of William Alexander Sivewright, glass maker, who had become a traveller for the company. But the situation changed when John Thomas Haden Richardson left his Stourbridge family's business, the Wordsley Glass Works, to join the company as manager in 1863. Ellis[107] states that Richardson joined the company as managing partner, but only the 1868 Post Office directory assigns him this status; the 1863 edition of the same directory lists him as manager, as does Robson's 1870 directory.[108]

J.T.H. Richardson came from one of the most creative and successful businesses in the trade, and was himself responsible for numerous innovations during his time at Tutbury, including a patent awarded in 1866 for '*an improvement in moulding or pressing glass*'.[109] Pressed glass clearly became part of the factory's production during Richardson's time (perhaps from an even earlier date—see Chapter 5), for designs were registered in 1864 and 1868;[110] a frosted, pressed bowl decorated with a star pattern and marked with the 1864 design number has recently come to light (Fig. 26).[111]

Richardson also took the lead in the introduction of novel machinery to the trade. In 1869, for example, he invented a shearing machine for cutting the tops of wine glasses, the subject of another patent, for '*an improved method of cutting flint glass…and in apparatus to be employed therefor*'.[112] His proposed introduction of this machine at Tutbury resulted in a dispute with the Flint Glassmakers' Friendly Society, which was eventually resolved via a compromise; the Union would not prevent its introduction but wanted to be able to negotiate the terms of its use (see Chapter 8).[113]

---

[106] Elton was described as manager of the glassworks on the marriage certificate of his daughter, Sarah Ann Elton, 3 Feb 1859.
[107] Ellis 2002, 335.
[108] *Harrod's Directory,* 1870, 1049.
[109] *London Gazette,* 7 Sep 1866, 4930.
[110] TNA: BT 43/61/170914; BT 43/61/217107-217109.
[111] 'Pressed glass bowl from Tutbury Glass Co.', *Glass Message Board,*
<http://www.glassmessages.com/ index.php?topic=49695.0>, accessed 29 Mar 2022.
[112] *London Gazette,* 12 Mar 1869, 599. This patent became void in 1872 because of non-payment of Stamp Duty: London Gazette, 8 Mar 1872, 1373.
[113] Matsumura 1976, 42-43.

**Fig. 26. A pressed and frosted glass bowl from the
Tutbury Glass Company.** The design, No. 170914, was
registered on 11 Jan 1864.

Under Richardson, the glassworks appears to have been efficiently run,
and productive. As a result of its isolated situation, the Tutbury works
could not expect to recruit skilled workmen locally, so from time to time
he advertised in the Birmingham newspapers. Glassblowers would have
had to be recruited through their Union in this period, unless there were no
unemployed available, so his notices were mostly for the less well-
organised cutters. In 1864, for example, he was looking for twelve flint
glass cutters[114] and for '*a first-class wine chair*', i.e., a complete
glassblowing team consisting of a workman, servitor, and footmaker,
skilled in making wine glasses. Basic wages were 34, 25, and 15 shillings,
respectively.[115] The cutters may have been needed, at least in part, to
replace men who had gone with William Alexander Sivewright to his new
glassworks in Hatton (see Chapter 7). The number of cutters increased
between 1861 and 1871, so in 1865 he advertised the factory's 10-hp steam

---

[114] *Aris's Birmingham Gazette,* 23 Apr 1864, 4.
[115] *Aris's Birmingham Gazette,* 3 Dec 1864, 4.

engine for sale '*on account of it being too small for the work required*'.[116] Richardson may also have been responsible for attempts to develop a new export market, not in the U.S.A. but in the British Empire; a Melbourne, Australia newspaper advertised the auction of a shipment of Tutbury glassware in 1870.[117]

In March 1866 Richardson advertised for a foreman cutter and for seven glass cutters, stating that he needed '*seven good and steady workmen, for permanent situations. None other will be engaged*'.[118] This time, in all likelihood, he was seeking to recruit strike breakers—a glass cutters' strike began in July 1865 at Dudley, but then spread to other regions, presumably including Tutbury. The strike continued for almost a year but ended in defeat for the workers.

Richardson may also have been the prime mover in the installation of a second furnace and glasshouse in the late 1860s. Following the Jacksons' 1880 liquidation of the business, the advertisement for the sale or lease of the works noted that they contained both a ten-pot and an eight-pot furnace (see Chapter 9). In 1869, in connection with the proposed introduction of a wine glass shearing machine at Tutbury, the Central Secretary of the FGMFS reported that: '*On the 18th of April, I received a request from the Tutbury District that I should go there, and see their employer, relative to a number of men he required to start the other furnace.*' A second chimney, seemingly emerging from a rectangular building rather than a cone, can be seen in Figs 18, 19, and 20, which date from the early twentieth century.

The second furnace may have been in the base of the chimney, which seems to have survived the rebuilding of the glasshouse itself; a photograph (Fig. 27) of glassblower Richard Bell (1900-1957; grandson of Benjamin Bell), perhaps from the mid-1930s, shows him at work in the final reincarnation of the glass house, but in front of what appears to be a furnace within the base of a chimney. By the later 1940s, however, no chimney was to be seen emerging from either the cone or the adjacent glasshouse (Fig. 23), and a postwar painting of glassblower Harry Hassent at work depicts him in front of a clearly different furnace (Fig. 28).

In 1871, Richardson was living on Burton Street, Tutbury, in the large house adjacent to the glassworks (later known as Southernhey) and was described as a flint glass manufacturer employing 53 men, 38 youths, and

---

[116] *Birmingham Daily Post*, 28 Oct 1865, 2.
[117] *Melbourne Argus (Victoria, Australia)*, 17 May 1870, 2.
[118] *Birmingham Daily Post*, 1 Mar 1866, 4; Aris's Birmingham Gazette, 31 Mar 1866, 3.

6 women. The 64-year-old James Elton had retired and was living at Park Cottage, at the junction of Park Lane and Castle Street, Tutbury. Thomas Small had died in London in 1867 at the age of 37, and the position of clerk was now filled by Richard Banks Stevens, 24, from Stourbridge. Although most of the workforce still described themselves as glass blowers and makers or as cutters and roughers, Richardson had advertised for a glass engraver in 1863 and again in 1867, and by 1871 had established a small group of engravers led by a young Bohemian glass engraver, Friedrich (Frederick) August Bohm. The remaining members of the group were young local recruits who presumably were being taught engraving skills by Bohm.

Fig. 27. Glassblower Richard Bell (1900-1957) at work, 1930s. The furnace appears to be within a chimney that is older than the building housing it.

61

Fig. 28. Painting, 'Harry Hassent and No. 8 Pot'
by Geoffrey Hulme. Collection of Tutbury Museum.

Very soon after the census of 1871, Richardson left the partnership with the Jacksons to start his own glassworks, the Castle Flint Glass Works (later the Royal Castle Glass Works), just across the River Dove in Hatton, Derbyshire. The occupational description and number of employees for Richardson in the census record (taken 2 April 1871) clearly refer to the Tutbury Glass Company, but by June 27 of the same year he was advertising for a glass packer for the Castle Flint Glass Works.[119] The reasons for his departure are unknown; there may have been disagreements over strategy with the Jackson family or other causes of deterioration in their relationship, or he may simply have wanted the opportunity to create a new enterprise and hire a workforce on his own terms. The availability of a relatively new glassworks in Hatton, unoccupied since the 1868 bankruptcy of Sivewright & Son (see Chapter 7), likely provided the right opportunity at the right time. He took Bohm and many other employees with him.

---

[119] *Birmingham Daily Post,* 27 Jun 1871, 4.

William Alexander Sivewright and the Flint Glass Makers' Friendly Society

By the 1850s, both glassmakers and glasscutters had formed unions. The earliest country-wide union of glassmakers, the United Flint Glass Makers' Society, was founded in 1844, but was bankrupted by an unsuccessful strike in 1848. It was reorganised in 1849 as the Flint Glass Makers' Friendly Society (FGMFS), and delegates from Tutbury participated in the reorganisation meeting in Manchester in September 1849 and in the first annual conference held in 1850 in Birmingham.[120] There were 23 to 24 members of the FGMFS at Tutbury throughout the 1850s; at three members per chair (takers-in were not eligible to join the society), this implies close to 100% membership for four chairs and two shifts. The first full Roll of Members of the Society appeared in the Flint Glass Makers' Magazine in May 1856, with a total national membership of 1,060 glass makers. A membership certificate for the FGMFS is shown in Fig. 29.

One of the delegates to the 1849 meeting from Tutbury was William Alexander Sivewright (or Sievewright), a man from the classic nineteenth-century mould of union activist and local preacher. He was born in Newcastle-on-Tyne in 1811 and came to Tutbury via London in the late 1830s, possibly encouraged by advertisements such as the one mentioned previously, suggesting that *'Serious professors of religion would find this a comfortable place'*. Sivewright was a leading figure in the FGMFS over the early years of its history, serving as its first Central Secretary (CS) up to 1852 and then again from 1860-63. As a result, the Tutbury District, small in membership compared to the major glassmaking centres of Stourbridge, Birmingham, South Lancashire, South Yorkshire, Newcastle, Glasgow, and Edinburgh, enjoyed a disproportionate prominence in the Society's affairs.

---

[120] Matsumura 1983, 85-89.

The FGMFS soon established itself as a successful protector of its members' interests, and glass makers came to be regarded as part of the Victorian 'Labour Aristocracy'. Much of the Society's influence and effectiveness came about through the publication of its quarterly journal, the *Flint Glass Makers' Magazine* (FGMM), the quality and longevity of which was later held up as a model of its type by Sidney and Beatrice Webb and other trades union historians. William Gillinder, Birmingham District Secretary, edited the magazine from 1850-52, and thereafter the role was taken on by the Central Secretary, including Sivewright during his second term of office. The high standard of literacy exhibited by a significant number of factory workers, writing letters and articles in their spare time, is quite unexpected, though there may have been a fair degree of sub-editing by the Central Secretary. The opening address of the first Journal, in autumn 1850, probably had input from both Gillinder and Sivewright:

> To the Glass-Makers of England, Ireland and Scotland. Brothers,
> - In undertaking the management of the Magazine, we feel the trust
> reposed in us... We have advocated the wisdom of having a Journal
> for our Trade for years, not from feelings of ambition or pride, but
> simply from the knowledge of the power of the press; it is a
> powerful engine that Glass-makers have never called to their
> assistance in battling with the giant Capital for the rights of
> Labour.[121]

An almost complete series of the FGMM from 1850 to 1903 has survived in the Modern Records Centre at the University of Warwick. It provides a rich resource of information on trade union history in general and the issues and conditions that prevailed in the glassmaking industry in particular, as well as membership details relating to the Tutbury (and later Hatton) factories contained in the District's quarterly financial returns.

The constitution of the FGMFS was not exactly a model of democracy and corporate governance. The Central Secretary was elected each year by a vote of all members, but he then single-handedly managed the Society's affairs with the support of a Central Committee (CC) which he nominated himself. The executive powers of the Society were technically vested in this committee but, in practice, and perhaps for valid practical reasons, the Central Secretary would generally pick his committee from fellow workers in his own factory or district, who might do little more than rubber-stamp

---

[121] FGMM, 1850, Vol. 1, 1. MRC: 126/YG/F/4/1/1.

his actions. The closing statement of the retiring Central Committee in Sivewright's last year as Central Secretary in 1863 was addressed from Tutbury, in the names of John Donkin, Joseph Price, Thomas Watson, Philip McGuiness, Benjamin Smart, and Edward Bentley—all Tutbury men.

Fig. 29. A membership certificate for the Flint Glass Makers' Friendly Society (FGMFS).

The other side of the coin of this concentration of power in one man's hands was the immense dedication and energy required to carry out the central secretary's duties while holding down a full-time glassblower's job. Sivewright was the first in a line of talented and committed central secretaries, who were undoubtedly another major factor in the success of the Society. The demands of the role were daunting—editorship and production of the journal, consolidation of the quarterly financial returns from more than 20 local district secretaries of differing levels of competence, travelling the country to negotiate in local and national disputes, mediation between different factions within the Society which sometimes split into West Midlands and North of England camps on major issues, organisation of national conferences in an era of limited communication, formulation of union policy in the context of restrictive legislation and hostile employers, and much more. The central secretary's remuneration for his toils was a princely £5 per quarter, equivalent to about £500 in 2020 (based on the Retail Price Index).

In his closing address as Central Secretary in 1863, Sivewright stated:

> *Fellow Tradesmen: In resigning the office of CS, I beg to thank the Trade generally, and the District Secretaries in particular, for that kindness and consideration they have manifested towards me. In taking my leave of the Society, with which I have been connected, in all its varied circumstances, for a period of upwards of 36 years, I may be allowed to express a hope that whatever differences of opinion may have arisen (and in some cases no doubt unavoidably) on any subject connected with the Society, that everyone will look upon such differences, as I do; recognize the right of every man to form his own opinions, and, if needs be, to disseminate them, but without personal ill will to others.* [122]

Sivewright does not appear to have been very adept in monetary affairs. The first report of William Gillinder, who took over from him as Central Secretary in 1852, stressed the need for an improvement in the Society's financial systems. While this was directed mainly at the district secretaries, there is, perhaps, some implied criticism of Sivewright as well. Indeed, it was only from the time of Gillinder's appointment that detailed quarterly returns from districts were published in the Society's magazine, providing FGMFS members with data enabling them to monitor their union's

---

[122] FGMM, 1863, Vol. 4, 737. MRC: 126/YG/F/4/1/2

financial stewardship and health. Sivewright's second successor as Central Secretary in 1863, Benjamin Smart of Glasgow, was also critical of the state of the financial records he inherited, reporting errors amounting to £153 13s 4d in Sivewright's accounting, which the latter acknowledged. The temptation of embezzlement was an occupational hazard for officers of friendly societies, trade unions, and similar associations in the nineteenth century, but in this case it was much more likely a question of negligence. Sivewright's mind may have been distracted by his forthcoming commercial enterprise or the deaths of his daughters Anne and Martha in 1860 and 1862 respectively. But it is noticeable that, while other retiring central secretaries were almost invariably feted with presentations, dinners, and praise for their dedication and contribution to the Society, there was nothing similar reported for Sivewright. Perhaps the slight financial bad taste, combined with his 'swapping sides' (see below), resulted in the Union stalwart not getting the plaudits he may have deserved for his efforts of 36 years.

Sivewright has also been ignored by subsequent historians. The whereabouts of back copies of the FGMM were unknown for a period of 40 years until their rediscovery in 1972. They were then used by Takao Matsumura as the prime source for a 1976 University of Warwick PhD thesis, later published in revised and reconstructed form. It provides an admirably researched picture of the trade and the Society. But, inexplicably, it completely ignores Sivewright as the founding Central Secretary from 1850. Gillinder is referred to erroneously as the first secretary, with credit for almost all the Society's early success. Sivewright is mentioned only once, in regard to his role in negotiating the outcome of the 1858/59 lockout (below), and nothing at all is said of his second term as Central Secretary from 1860-3. However, there are several references in the early pages of the magazine that make clear that 'W.A.S.' at Tutbury was operating as central secretary of the society at the time. Gillinder himself, writing as Birmingham District Secretary in 1851, referred to a meeting at which *'the CS and one of the CC attended from Tutbury'*, and in August 1852 he claimed eleven shillings expenses for a *'journey to Tutbury to settle books with late CS'*. On more than one occasion over the succeeding century, Tutbury had reason to feel it was unjustifiably treated as a poor relation of its West Midlands peers in the industry, but Matsumura's writing Sivewright out of history is particularly unfortunate. As much as anyone, he re-established the Union after 1849 and helped set the standard for the well-informed, literate debate that was the basis for the

FGMM's reputation over five decades.

A full-time job and involvement in union affairs did not stop Sivewright from playing a wider part in village life. In the 1854 Post Office Directory of Staffordshire, he is listed as a glassmaker, but also as a grocer and provision dealer in High Street. The 1861 census records him as a *'Glass Maker and Local Preacher'*, whilst Kelly's Post Office Directory of the same year lists *'William Sivewright, stationer and postmaster, High Street'.*[123] It may well be that the retail and post office businesses were nominally in his name but run by his wife and/or children.

Tutbury's relatively high profile in the administration of the FGMFS was not matched by any great militancy in its local labour relations. On the contrary, the records portray it as a haven of relative calm, with little unemployment, no evident strikes and steady union membership. Just once in the 1850s, in December 1859, the Central Committee reported:

> *Our trade still continues in a peaceful and prosperous position, little has occurred during the past quarter out of the ordinary routine of business, except at Tutbury, where a dispute has taken place about servitors' and footmakers' wages, these being very low indeed, and after a little agitation upon the question, eleven succeeded in obtaining 2s per week advance, with proportionate overwork.*[124]

The infrequency of 'agitation' may reflect a combination of William Sivewright's diplomatic presence, a light hand from the management in the years under Mrs Jackson's ownership, and the apparently uncompetitive marketplace, both for business and labour, that Tutbury occupied in comparison to the larger centres of glass manufacture in the West Midlands, North of England and Scotland. It is only under J.T.H. Richardson's more dynamic management of the Tutbury and Hatton factories from the mid-1860s onwards that dissension in worker/manager relations becomes evident.

The most damaging national dispute arose in 1858, when a strike began at two Stourbridge factories that then spread and eventually turned into a nationwide (but incomplete) lockout of glassmakers. The Tutbury glassmakers do not appear to have been locked out, since the Tutbury District quarterly return for February 1859 shows no payments for lost time, unlike those districts that were at the centre of the dispute. The

---

[123] *Kelly's Post Office Directory of Staffordshire,* 1861, 675-676.
[124] FGMM, 1859, Vol 3, 591. MRC: 126/YG/F/4/1/2.

lockout lasted for six months, from October 1858 until April 1859, and only ended when both sides had exhausted their funds. Sivewright played a key role in attempts to find common ground and was a participant in a meeting between the employers and the FGMFS on 4 April 1859 that ended the strike and lockout on terms favourable to the union.[125] As W.H. Packwood, then Central Secretary, recalled in 1877:

> *W.A. Sivewright of Tutbury, who contributed good and timely service to his fellow workers and the trade, and whose name should be forever remembered with the greatest respect, saw that it was necessary that some new ground should be made to work upon, that a fresh opening should be made somewhere, and he, unknown to anyone, set himself to revise our laws, and take away, or modify all that appeared obnoxious in them; this being done, he made known his intentions, and explained his views at large meetings in Stourbridge and Birmingham, which resulted in the Executivecalling a Conference [on 11 March at Birmingham]... The revised rules were discussed, and in the main accepted ... The resolutions being submitted to the trade, they bore the joint signatures of the Chairman, W.A. Sivewright, and the CS, J.W.Woolley, and established the groundwork upon which the strike was settled.[126]*

The employers agreed to meet to discuss revised rules. The Society felt that it was essential that Sivewright was present at the meeting:

> *It was then that I was sent off about dusk, and found myself late on a dark night, after walking from Burton, and the first time at Tutbury, and well received by Mr Sivewright. We talked matters over, and came to the conclusion and felt a relief that the end of the struggle was so close at hand. We rose early, it was a lovely spring and clear morning, everything seemed gay, the trees were putting forth new life, and as T. Watson made up the trio we seemed to be inspired with new sensations and partook of the gaiety around us. We arrived in Dudley in time to take part in the Meeting.[127]*

Agreement was readily reached, the new rules adopted, and the West Midlands Lockout ended.

---

[125] Matsumura 1983, 140.
[126] FGMM, 1877, Vol 9, 665-6. MRC: 126/YG/F/4/1/4.
[127] Ibid.

During Sivewright's second term of office, he initiated the concept of a national gathering of glass makers and their wives, the first of which was held at Belle Vue, Manchester on 2 August 1861, with Sivewright presiding at the dinner for 500 participants that evening.[128]

In the summer of 1863, as his term came to an end, Sivewright made a dramatic change in direction, exchanging a lifetime as an employee and union activist for the chance to become an entrepreneur himself. He left the Tutbury Glass Company and went into business in partnership with his son, William Jr, trading as W.A. Sivewright & Son, Flint Glass Manufacturers. Sivewright's venture, with its threat of competition for skilled labour and for a share of the local and regional markets, must have seriously concerned the Jacksons, and may perhaps have been a factor in their decision to recruit J.T.H. Richardson.

Although no direct evidence has yet come to light, there is little doubt that Sivewright's new venture was the first establishment of a glassworks alongside the North Staffordshire Railway in Scropton Lane, Hatton, the village adjoining Tutbury across the River Dove—the site which over the following hundred years operated variously as the Royal Castle Glassworks, Corbett & Co Ltd and, after the Second World War, the Trent Valley Glassworks. In 1969 Mr Frank Pegg, who had worked as an engineering fitter at the works from the turn of the century, passed on his recollections of the origins of the factory to Mr W.H. Bennett, then managing director of Trent Valley. Mr Pegg stated that *'The Hatton Works were built for a Mr Sivewright and used by him for the manufacture of tableware'*.[129]

Hatton was little more than a hamlet in the nineteenth century and, despite being in a different county, Derbyshire, was treated effectively as part of Tutbury for most purposes—the naming of its station as Tutbury Station being the most enduring example. The Hatton glassworks, in its various guises, was therefore frequently referred to by outsiders as 'Tutbury Glassworks' and in many sources is not distinguished from and often confused with the Ludgate Street, Tutbury factory. Not that there was any confusion locally; the Hatton works, by the river, was known as the 'Bottom Shop' and the Ludgate Street factory as the 'Top Shop'.

It may have taken some time for the Sivewrights' new works to get off the ground. The Tutbury District FGMFS membership numbers were unchanged in 1864 from their historic level of around 24. It was only in

---

[128] FGMM, 1861, Vol. 4, 285. MRC: 126/YG/F/4/1/2.
[129] Typescript, Tutbury Museum, ref. GL274h.

1865 that they increased to 36, and then to over fifty in 1866/67. Unfortunately, William and his son soon ran into financial difficulties and were declared bankrupt on 26 May 1868.[130] Their glassmaking operation closed. The impact can be seen clearly in the unemployment rolls of the FGMFS. Until that time, the Tutbury District had averaged only two to three men per quarter out of work, but in the week of 30 June, seven workmen joined the unemployed list: Philip McGuiness, Benjamin Bell, Benjamin Smart, George Cooke, George Thompson, Richard Thompson, and William Baxendale. A week later, they were joined by another workman, William Davis, plus nine servitors and footmakers.

Within weeks the Society had found work for most of the unemployed men elsewhere in the country, in Birmingham, Stourbridge, St Helens, Edinburgh and Glasgow, though the long-term Tutbury residents among them eventually found their way back onto the Jacksons' payroll in Ludgate Street. While several of the men had been relative newcomers to the local industry, others (McGuiness, Bell, Smart, and Cooke) were Tutbury stalwarts, evidence that Sivewright had been able to take some of the Jacksons' best craftsmen with him after 1863. The numbers involved allow an estimation of the scale of the Hatton operation—eight workmen and their supporting teams, working four chairs per shift, probably from an eight-pot furnace. Tutbury District FGMFS membership dropped from 48 to 31 between May and August 1868, indicating that the Sivewright glass blowing operation was similar in scale to that in Ludgate Street. No evidence of the extent of cutting in Hatton has yet come to light. The Hatton factory appears to have remained closed from 1868 until its resurrection in 1871 in the hands of J.T.H. Richardson.

Following his bankruptcy in 1868, Sivewright continued to try and make a living in the industry and in 1871 was living on High Street, Tutbury, and trading as a glass merchant. William Alexander Sivewright died in 1872 aged 61 and was buried at St Mary's, Tutbury on 2 July. No memorial survives to one of the village's most noteworthy but hitherto forgotten figures.

No other Tutbury glass maker achieved comparable prominence in Union affairs. Sivewright appears to have acted as Tutbury District Secretary as well as Central Secretary in his first period of office and may have continued in the district role until Thomas Watson Sr was appointed in Autumn 1861. Watson (father of the young Thomas Watson who spoke

---

[130] *London Gazette*, 29 May 1868, 3097.

so poignantly to the Parliamentary Commission in 1865) had been the Tutbury delegate to the triennial FGMFS conferences held in Glasgow and London in 1855 and 1858 respectively. He was succeeded in 1865 by Edwin Bentley, followed in turn by Philip Maguiness in 1866, Charles Cook in 1867, Benjamin Bell in 1874, Edwin Bentley again briefly in 1875, and Arthur Turner later that year. Both Maguiness and Turner are listed in the FGMM as living in Hatton while acting as district secretary and were probably employed at the Hatton factory; a glass maker working a double six-hour shift would find even a mile's walk to and from work a significant inconvenience. Other Tutbury district members to play some role in FGMFS affairs were John Donkin as a proposed trustee of funds in 1854, Joseph Price in a similar role in 1864, and Richard Stevens, George Cooke, and Edward Downey as Manchester conference delegates in 1867, 1871 and 1874 respectively.

Few details have survived of the cutters' unionisation in the Victorian era. The United Flint Glass Cutters' Society was established in 1844, and the Tutbury cutters appear to have been members of this Society, at least from the 1850s. In 1859, for example, the Birmingham Daily Post reported on a meeting of working men in Nottingham at which a delegation of glass makers and cutters from Stourbridge, Birmingham and Tutbury asked for support for those who were locked out of employment.[131]

---

[131] *Birmingham Daily Post,* 10 Mar 1859, 2.

Chapter 8

The Impact of the FGMFS in Tutbury

The major issues that occupied the energies of the FGMFS changed little over the decades under review. While it acted as a Friendly Society providing unemployment, sickness, and later, superannuation benefits in return for members' contributions, it operated primarily to improve their wages and employment conditions through control of the labour-force numbers and working practices. The principal means to achieve this and the impact on the Tutbury district, as recorded in the *Flint Glass Makers' Magazine*, are outlined below.

Restriction of Apprentice Numbers. Limiting the use of boys as cheap labour was the focus of much dispute. As well as affecting the available work for men who had served their time, the charge was that apprentices were then frequently discarded by the employer at the end of their term when they qualified for a full wage. An early FGMM correspondent in 1851 wrote:

> *Evils of Apprentices: Sir. It is a strange anomaly, that while we are doing all we can as a body to remove the surplus labour of our trade, and to reduce it, we have never thought of stopping the supply. It is an acknowledged fact that there is [sic] places in our trade where they do nothing else but rear apprentices and turn them off (like so many old horses) when they are out of their time.*[132]

The writer went on to make a moral case for craftsmen to refuse to teach apprentices, as they were only doing themselves out of a job. In November 1853 the Tutbury district paid Benjamin Smart and William Sivewright junior 7s 8d *'for loss of work in resisting a boy'*—the curious wording reflecting the time spent negotiating with the Tutbury management about the taking on of a new apprentice. As in many industries, the only sure route to an apprenticeship was to follow one's father; William Sivewright Jr, Thomas Watson Jr, and his Meer cousins are Tutbury examples, and

---

[132] FGMM, 1851, Vol. 1, 51. MRC: 126/YG/F/4/1/1.

there were many more in later years.

Elimination of Tramping. 'Tramping' had traditionally been the last resort of unemployed men in the industry. The organisation of tramping was a key activity of many of the early artisan trade unions. In the absence of local work, a man would receive a document showing him to be a member in good standing of his Society and take to the road to other parts of the country to seek work in his trade. Arriving in a new town, he would present his credentials to the local district secretary at the 'house of call', usually a pub, receiving in exchange supper, lodging, perhaps beer and a tramping allowance, funded by the Society. If there was work to be had, he took it; if not he would move on, often having also looked to the charity of his fellow glassmakers in that area. In hard times men could cover many hundreds of miles in unsuccessful treks from one district to another. There is no evidence of Tutbury glassmakers 'going on the tramp' themselves, but as a convenient stopping point between the northern counties and the West Midlands, the village perhaps saw a good share of these not-always-welcome visitors in the years after Jackson's glasshouse was built in 1836. The FGMFS answer to tramping was to establish a formal system of directing unemployed members to vacancies in other locations.

Operation of a National Unemployed Register. A key element in the Society's effectiveness was the introduction of a register of unemployed members on a national level. District secretaries notified the central secretary of the names of their unemployed men. If a vacancy arose in a district, the local secretary would first seek a candidate in that district; in the absence of anyone suitable he would contact the central secretary who would then direct an unemployed man from elsewhere to take up the position, with the Society paying the man's travel expenses. The FGMFS successfully imposed this system in many factories, and it was the principal source of complaints from employers about the 'tyranny' of the Union. It is notable that J.T.H. Richardson's newspaper advertisements for workers were generally for the less strongly unionised cutters, and it is likely that he had to follow the FGMFS route for recruiting blowers. The beneficial side of the system has already been noted in the rapid placing of redundant Hatton workers in 1868, and the travel expense payments that appear regularly in the Tutbury district quarterly returns are evidence of a flow of men in and out of the locality as employment opportunities fluctuated.

Maintenance of a Closed Shop. The frequently justified antagonism of the Society towards bad employers was as nothing to the vitriol heaped upon fellow glassblowers who stayed outside the union. The 'Betrayers',

'Blacklegs', 'Black Rats', and 'Traitors', supposedly collaborating with rogue employers, were seen by their unionised colleagues as the weakest link in their attempts to improve oppressive working conditions. The FGMFS were generally successful in establishing a high level of membership in the larger glasshouses that used traditional handblowing methods, though it was more difficult where pressed production was in operation (requiring lesser skill levels), and in 'cribs', the one-workman set-ups, working just a small pot or two of mainly cullet-based mix, that came and went in many districts, usually attempting to eke out an existence below the radar of the Exciseman and the FGMFS. The near-100% membership in Tutbury has already been noted. In January 1857 the Central Secretary published the names of all 'non-society men' in the trade, and among 253 held out nationally for shame there is just one from Tutbury—'E. Kirkham, crib man'—though to be fair to him, Enoch Kirkham was listed as a Society member in both May 1856 and May 1857.

Emigration. Another weapon in trying to limit the labour supply was the financial encouragement of men to emigrate in times of recession in the home trade to North America or Australasia, where there were nascent glass industries. These programmes were generally acknowledged to have been failures; reports from overseas frequently made it clear that there was no easy life awaiting glassmakers in the promised lands. W.S. Gillinder, Sivewright's successor as Central Secretary, was a successful exception, trying his luck in the U.S.A. at the end of his term of office in 1854 and eventually becoming a pressed glass manufacturer in Philadelphia. There is a later, more typical Tutbury example in Charles James Cooke. Cooke was from an extended family of Jackson glassworkers and, after more than thirty years as a glassblower in the village, he sailed to New York in 1888 at the age of 43 with his wife Hannah and seven children. Arriving inauspiciously in a blizzard that closed the city down for several weeks, he failed to find employment as a glassmaker and turned his hand to working in a valve factory. Notwithstanding, the family established itself successfully in their new land and his present-day descendants have kept alive the story of their great-grandfather's Tutbury glassmaking roots.

Resistance to Technological Change. The FGMFS was intrinsically opposed to changes in working methods. Pressed glass technologies obviously caused major challenges. But in the traditional hand-blown glass houses, the Society's success in resisting major modifications to both the technical processes and the 'chair' system of labour organisation is evidenced by the survival of the original craft methods almost unchanged over two centuries from the late 1700s. While the FGMM contains several eloquent passages in theoretical support of the need to embrace the scientific and engineering advances of the period, in practice the Society frequently thwarted attempts by employers to introduce technological advances, through constraints on members' wages or working practices that effectively nullified the labour cost-savings implicit in the proposed innovations.

This is exemplified by the introduction of a wine-glass shearing machine by J.T.H. Richardson at the Tutbury works in 1869. T.J. Wilkinson, the Central Secretary, reported to members:

On the 18th of April, I received a request from the Tutbury District that I should go there, and see their employer, relative to a number of men he required to start the other furnace. Accordingly, on the 23rd and 24th I attended for that purpose; and the application he made was for one complete chair to make best wines, (straw stems) etc; also seven servitors and seven footmakers, 2nd class. These he intended to distribute in the following way - He had introduced and patented a small machine to supersede hand labour in the shearing of wines, goblets, etc. The machine is said to so lessen the labour of a workman in the production of each individual article, that it will enable him to make as many as two servitors and two footmen can produce. Consequently he intends to so place the workmen he now has at the two furnaces together with the seven servitors and footmen now applied for, as well as those already engaged, by aid of the said machine.[133]

This caused considerable alarm in the union, as it promised to radically alter the traditional composition of the 'chair', and a heavyweight delegation was despatched to Tutbury to '*lay down the conditions of working*'. The conditions they demanded were:

That no member of our society be dismissed to make room for a machine, and that the machinist be a member of our society, but recommend that a workman be employed to work the machine. That the present rate of numbers be strictly adhered to, and no servitor or footmaker be compelled to blow more, as the machine is no assistance to their department.

The delegation was able to report back that:

---

[133] FGMM, 1869, Vol. 6, 580. University of Warwick Library, Microform Section.

> *When they waited upon Mr. Richardson, after a long interview he*
> *agreed to all the conditions except one, and that was the one in*
> *reference to employing members of our Society as machinists, and*
> *the ultimate settlement of that point was, that requiring two men to*
> *work the machine, he agreed as a preliminary arrangement that*
> *we should select one and he the other. Accordingly he chose a man*
> *he had in his employ, and we chose an unemployed man as the*
> *other...We must acknowledge in justice to Mr. Richardson that the*
> *open and considerate manner, as also for the trouble and pains he*
> *took to show to the delegates the working and capabilities of his*
> *machine, was deserving of our best thanks.*[134]

The new invention seems not to have got off the ground, perhaps because of the conditions imposed, and five years later W.S. Packwood, the then Central Secretary, was able to muse in his editorial:

> *MACHINERY ...I have often thought that if strong opposition had*
> *been given to the attempt to introduce the Shearing Machine at*
> *Tutbury, that the indignation of the whole of the employers of this*
> *trade, and probably some in other branches, would have been*
> *roused against us, and the very thing brought into existence by our*
> *stupid determination to push it out; but by allowing it free*
> *exercise, with proper regard to the protection of our positions, it*
> *is now, I think, an attempt of the past, and it will be many years*
> *before it makes its appearance again.*[135]

Fellowship and Relaxation. Over the years, Birmingham-based FGMFS officials seemed ever willing to travel to Tutbury to solve local problems. They may have had motives going beyond fears that Tutbury's parochial concerns might have national ramifications. Perhaps a day out in the Dove Valley's fresh air, with time and expenses paid, offered a welcome respite from the grime and pollution of their West Midlands base. This was exemplified as far back as 1851, and on a much larger scale, when the FGMM included an address from the Committee of Birmingham Flint Glass Makers to the Flint Glass Makers of Yorkshire, Manchester, Warrington, St Helens and Longport:

> *It was unanimously resolved at our full meeting that we should*
> *have an excursion to Tutbury, to take place in the early part of*

---

[134] Ibid, 583.
[135] FGMM, 1874, Vol. 4, 1. MRC: 126/YG/F/4/1/4.

July. It was also resolved that we should invite the Glass-makers of the above-named places to meet us there, and have a festive gathering of Glass-makers such as was never before witnessed. To accomplish our aims at as light an expense as possible, we have determined to save a penny per week out of our drink money towards defraying the expenses.

We think the monster gathering would tend to unite us stronger to each other in the bonds of union; and while we contemplate a day's enjoyment, we will not forget our wives and sweethearts; let them share our enjoyment as well as our hardships and sorrows. The scenery is beautiful; Tutbury is situated on and between two hills. The views from the hills are splendid; the peaks of Derbyshire are seen in the far distance, and a beautiful country visible to the eye for twenty miles stretches around, and it is in reality one of the most beautiful views in England. On one of the hills at Tutbury stands the castle, now in ruins, dating its existence to the Saxon era; it is rendered famous in history as being the prison of Mary Queen of Scots; its ruin is ascribed to that famous destroyer of feudal strongholds, Oliver Cromwell. We have the free use of the castle and grounds, to hold our fete in... The contrast will be great, but none the less pleasing that Labour's sons and daughters shall enjoy the festive dance and joyous song where formerly our Saxon forefathers bled and died for liberty, where royalty was imprisoned, and where the death-blow was struck at serfdom in Britain. Everything in the locality will tend to our enjoyment; and lastly, but not least, the moral effect of the gathering will be great – it will show our unity; it will tend to bring us as a body in close connexion with each other, and establish a lasting bond of friendship and unity amongst us. Let all hands, then, begin to prepare for it. Let it be a monster gathering. Let us begin to view the beauties of nature and take advantage of science to make it minister to our pleasure.[136]

There is no record of a gathering taking place; it apparently fell victim to the financial problems caused by strike and lockout action at the time.

The Intangible Impact of the FGMFS. There were other less visible effects of the activities of the Society that would nevertheless have had profound effects on the lives of the glassmakers and on their communities.

---

[136]FGMM, 1851, Vol. 1, 84. MRC: 126/YG/F/4/1/1

Participation in this small but highly effective union must have helped its members attain some level of self-confidence. Some learned to speak publicly, to negotiate with local management, and to gain the support of their fellow glassmakers. Others learned to write for the FGMM and other publications. These skills could be put to good use in other environments too: in Church, Chapel, or the Friendly Societies' lodges. In Tutbury, the glassmakers and cutters were the stalwarts of the local lodge of the Oddfellows, the Loyal Sir Oswald Mosley Lodge. They were proud of their craft, proud of their skills, and proud of their place as members of the Labour Aristocracy (Fig. 30).

Fig. 30. A picture of self-confidence: the Labour Aristocracy at work.
There is no provenance for this photograph, from Tutbury Museum's collection, but it was probably taken at the Tutbury glassworks. It shows one shift of glassmakers: four chairs (workman, servitor, and footman) and four boys working as takers-in (plus one extra adult, perhaps the teazer, as the furnace fireman was called). Some of the men are wearing high-waisted trousers and wooden-soled clogs, suggestive of a relatively early date for the image.

Chapter 9

The End of the Jackson Era

Little is known of the management of the Tutbury works after Richardson's departure. Jabez Elton is listed as manager in 1872, but by 1874 he had been replaced by John Edwin Green.[137] The managers inherited a difficult situation, which only became worse as the decade progressed. First, Eleanor Jackson died in December 1874 aged 73, leaving her two daughters, Caroline and Mary Ann Jackson, as sole partners in the company. Then, beginning in 1876/7, a major depression hit the trade nationwide; by 1879, approximately a quarter of the total membership of the FGMFS was unemployed.[138] Conditions were so bad that in 1879 the glass makers agreed to a cut in wages.[139] In Tutbury, the outcome was that the Jackson sisters could not meet their debts. The Tutbury Flint Glass Company (as it was then called) went into voluntary liquidation at the beginning of 1880; notices of general meetings of creditors '*In the matter of Proceedings for Liquidation by Arrangement or Composition with Creditors, instituted by Caroline Jackson and Mary Anne Jackson...*' were announced in the London Gazette.[140] Efforts were made to sell the business. In February the London Standard advertised:

> *FLINT GLASS TRADE - To be LET or SOLD, the TUTBURY FLINT GLASS WORKS, consisting of one ten-pot and one eight-pot furnace, engine, boiler, and shafting in good working order; two cutting shops, cratemaker's shop with circular saw, engraving, roughing and blacksmith's shop, office, show-room, warehouse, packing-room &c. The eight-pot furnace has its fires in, and can be started at once. - Apply the Tutbury Glass Works, Burton-on-Trent.*[141]

Two months later, the stock was advertised at knock-down prices in the Derby Mercury:

---

[137] *Wright's Directory of South Derbyshire,* 1874, 267.
[138] Matsumura 1976, 96.
[139] Ibid., 223-228.
[140] *London Gazette,* 20 Jan 1880, 320; 10 Feb 1880, 661.
[141] *London Standard,* 26 Feb 1880, 8.

> *The TUTBURY GLASS COMPANY, to effect a clearance at once of their splendid TABLE and other GLASS, have GREATLY REDUCED their PRICES, and will commence SELLING on MONDAY next, April 12th, for a limited period only. Innkeepers, Confectioners and Housekeepers generally will do well to embrace this opportunity. Intending purchasers are requested to pay an early visit.*[142]

Attempts to sell the business as a going concern failed, and it closed its doors. The Jackson sisters may have lost some assets in the liquidation, but they were certainly not destitute. At census time in 1881 they were still living in the family home on High Street and had one resident domestic servant. They still described themselves as retired glass manufacturers. Caroline died on 22 December 1882 at the age of 62, leaving a personal estate valued at ninety-two pounds, twelve shillings and ten pence.[143]

Mary Ann survived for another 30 years. In 1884 she left Tutbury; the house on High Street was sold by auction on 6 May 1884, and the contents on 16 May.[144] She went to live in Southport, Lancashire as companion and chaperone to two step-nieces, Fanny and May Sheldon, whose parents had died recently. They were the daughters of the Rev. Richard Vincent Sheldon, elder brother of Frederick Sheldon and son of Eleanor Jackson's sister. A Cambridge graduate, Richard Sheldon was Vicar of Ormskirk, Lancashire. His wife died in 1878 and he in 1884. He left a personal estate of just under £2,000, apparently sufficient for his daughters to live on their own means with four servants in 1891. May Sheldon married the Rev. John Bevan in 1894; he became Vicar of Slad, Gloucestershire in the same year. Fanny Sheldon and Mary Ann Jackson followed the couple to Gloucestershire and took a house near them in Uplands; Mary Ann Jackson died there in 1912.

The failure of the Tutbury Glass Company was not the end of the Jackson family's involvement with glassmaking. In a surprising turn of events, William Henry Congreve Jackson (1859-1945), eldest son of the Rev. William Henry Jackson, became an agent for Thomas Webb and Sons of the Dennis Glassworks, Stourbridge, and eventually took charge of the firm's London office. After the retirement of the last of the Webbs in 1900, he became managing director and continued in that position until 1920.

---

[142] *Derby Mercury,* 7 Apr 1880, 4.
[143] SRO: Will of Caroline Jackson, Probate 21 Jun 1884.
[144] *Derby Mercury,* 30 Apr 1884, 1; 14 May 1884, 1.

Chapter 10

An Interlude: The Tutbury Flint Glass Co. Ltd 1880-1906

The Jacksons' bankruptcy was the end of their involvement in glass making in Tutbury, but not the end of the glassworks, for in December of 1880 it was announced that:

> *The Tutbury Glass Company Ltd has been registered with a capital of £7500 in 500 shares of £15 each. Its objects are to carry on the business of glass manufacturers and cutters. The promoters are Sir T. Mosley, Bart., and R.A. Eadie [Eddie], Burton-on-Trent; W.J. Smith, Derby; T. Brown and J. Elton, of Tutbury; and W. Wayte, Burton-on-Trent.*[145]

Also in December, a report of the distribution of Christmas gifts to the poor by the trustees of Wakefield's Charity noted that Sir Tonman Mosley (senior trustee) '*in opening the proceedings referred to the reopening of the glass works, which he hoped would put labour and wages within the reach of many who had been debarred since the old glass works closed'.*[146] This announcement must have brought some relief to many who had been struggling; the same report noted that the Charity was distributing about 80 gallons of soup to the poor of Tutbury twice a week.

Sir Tonman Mosley (1813-90) was the driving force in relaunching the works. The Mosleys were the most significant resident local landowners, their family seat at Rolleston Hall being little more than a mile away. Tonman, the third baronet, succeeded his father, Sir Oswald, author of the 1832 history of Tutbury in which the most-quoted early reference to the glass factory is recorded. Tonman was followed by three further Sir Oswalds, the last of whom, his great-grandson, the sixth baronet, extended his horizons well beyond rural Staffordshire and gained notoriety as the founder of the British Union of Fascists in the 1930s. No portrait of Sir Tonman has been discovered, the only known image of him being as an indistinct figure seated with his tenants from Rolleston, Needwood and

---

[145] *Furniture Gazette,* 11 Dec 1880, 366.
[146] *Derby Mercury,* 29 Dec 1880, 8.

Tutbury in connection with a dinner he gave in 1873 to celebrate the restoration of Rolleston Hall after a disastrous fire, and the marriage of his eldest son, Oswald (Fig. 31).

Fig 31. Sir Tonman Mosley and his tenants at Rolleston Hall, 1873.
Mosley is wearing a grey suit and is seated in the front row, in front of the inner left column.

The early baronets can be credited with playing active philanthropic roles in both Rolleston and Tutbury. Among many examples, Tonman's position as senior trustee of Wakefield's Charity has already been mentioned, and his father sponsored the establishment in 1834 of the first Friendly Society branch in Tutbury, the 'Loyal Sir Oswald Mosley Lodge' of the Manchester Unity of Oddfellows. By 1880 both organisations were playing a vital part in providing a minimal welfare relief net to villagers left close to destitution by age, illness, or unemployment. It is fair to speculate that philanthropic motives played a part, as much as commercial enterprise, in Sir Tonman's efforts to rescue Tutbury's largest employer. Certainly, the modest size of the factory, together with the depressed state of the glass industry and the economy in general, hardly combined to create an exciting investment opportunity of significance to a man of his wealth.

Nevertheless, Mosley persuaded his contacts in the district, both gentry and industrialists, to chip in as shareholders of a new company, the Tutbury Flint Glass Company Ltd. Of the authorised share capital of 500 £15 shares, some 413 had been issued by the time of the first shareholder listing that is known, dated 14 October 1882—representing a total of £6,195 initial capital. Mosley himself was the largest subscriber, with 85 shares, and he was joined by a rather glittering local list of 'the great and the good'. Amongst well-known family names were James Arkwright of Cromford, Richard Bott of Church Broughton, William Curzon of Alvaston, and William Joseph Smith of Dove Cliffe. Most notable however were the representatives of almost all the leading Burton-on-Trent brewing concerns: Samuel Allsopp, Michael Bass, Sydney Evershed, Richard Eddie and William Wayte of John Marston & Sons, Salt & Co., Thompson & Son, and William Worthington. The full shareholder register across the period is shown in Table 2. The preponderance of brewing interests may be no more than a reflection of that industry's dominant position in the local economy. But it may be that the brewers' investments were motivated at least in part by their desire to protect a local source of supply of glassware for their growing network of tied public houses.

The new company took over the trading concern and assets of the works, its objective being '*to carry on the business of glass manufacturers and cutters*'. There are no records to show whether any consideration was paid by the company to the Jackson sisters for the assets of the business in 1880. No financial accounts are to be found in the Companies House filings for the Tutbury Flint Glass Company Ltd[147], now held by the National Archive, though with such a widespread group of private shareholders it is possible that some papers remain to come to light.

The freehold of the Ludgate Street factory was held by Henry Jackson in 1840[148] and was in the hands of the Jackson family at the time of their business's closure. In the abortive offering in February 1880 the '*Works*' were advertised as to be '*sold or let*'. The new company purchased the business assets, but not the freehold of the factory building and land. That

---

[147] The company is variously referred to in different documents as the Tutbury Flint Glass Company Ltd., the Tutbury Glass Company Ltd., and the Tutbury Glass Works Company Ltd. There is no indication that it ever formally changed its name.
[148] TNA: IR 29/32/217. Digital version:
<http://freepages.genealogy.rootsweb.ancestry.com/~laetoli/tutbury titheapportionment.html>, accessed 29 Mar 2022.

was conveyed to Sir Tonman by deed on 30 October 1880,[149] presumably as part of Sir Tonman's efforts to save the situation, and then leased to the company. The parties to the conveyance were the Rev. William Henry Jackson, Caroline Jackson, and Mary Ann Jackson, as heirs of Eleanor Jackson, Mosley himself, William Small (a solicitor living at Cliff House, Tutbury, son of Thomas Small by his first wife and stepson of Martha Small, Eleanor's sister), and Robert Shirley Belcher, a retired surgeon from Burton-on-Trent. Small and Belcher may have held mortgages on the premises. The earliest surviving lease document is dated 10 September 1894 between Sir Oswald Mosley (the fourth baronet, after Tonman's death in 1890) as Lessor and the Tutbury Flint Glass Co Ltd as Lessee, for a period of 21 years at an annual rent of £125. This lease was granted in consideration of the surrender of an earlier one dated 10 July 1881. It relates to:

> *All that parcel...in Ludgate Street and Burton Street Tutbury delineated in the map drawn at the end and coloured blue together with the Glass Manufactory Counting Houses storerooms messuage dwelling house workshops offices and all other erections and buildings upon the same piece of land and the Engine Room and Boiler thereon, now in the occupation of the Lessees.*

As had been the case with Mrs Jackson and her daughters, Mosley and his fellow shareholders were dependent on retaining capable professional management. The company hired Thomas Brown as manager; he had been clerk for a Manchester glass manufacturer before moving to Tutbury. The 1881 census lists Brown, aged 41, as manager, and Jabez Elton, the manager back in 1872, as clerk. Brown and Elton were in the same roles on the 1891 census. Entries in the Post Office/Kelly's Trade Directories of 1884, 1888, and 1892 confirm Brown's role as manager, but later editions indicate that he was replaced by Jabez Elton some time before 1896; in fact, Elton gave his occupation as manager of the Tutbury Glass Company on the marriage certificate of his daughter in December 1891. He appears to have remained in that role until the company's closure.

Employee numbers in the Ludgate Street factory can be estimated at about 50 through most of the period from 1881 to the turn of the century. Entries in the 1901 census, at which time the Royal Castle Glass Works in

---

[149] Referenced in SRO: Will of Sir Tonman Mosley, Bart., Probate 30 June 1890.

Hatton was closed, indicate that the company employed a roughly equal number of glass cutters and glass blowers/makers, perhaps around 20 of each, plus about ten ancillary workers. These numbers indicate a mixed product range of both decorated and undecorated glassware; a business focused solely on high-quality cut glass would normally require a preponderance of cutters as opposed to blowers.

To date, no evidence (invoices, ledgers, etc.) has come to light to reveal the level of trading between the Tutbury glassworks and the Burton breweries, though anecdotally there are statements by management in the glassworks' publicity literature of the 1950s that the mainstay of the business prior to Thomas Webb & Corbett's acquisition in 1905 was the supply of functional glassware to the brewery trade. One trade publication goes as far as to say the factory *'had, hitherto, been exclusively engaged in making glass in the form of jugs, tumblers. Etc., for the licensed victuallers' trade'.*[150] But occasional press reports through the 1880s give evidence of a continuing production of decorated tableware - for example: *'LITTLEOVER FLOWER SHOW. The Tutbury Glass Company exhibited for sale a collection of their celebrated flower vases, for which, we imagine, there must be a large demand.'*[151] Other notices, from 1884 and 1886 respectively, mention *'a first-class display of flower stands and ornamental glass'*[152] and *'An exhibition of cut, fancy and other glass.*[153]

Documentary evidence across the twenty-five years of the Tutbury Flint Glass Company's operation is scanty. The fragmentary impression, perhaps false, is of a modest business going nowhere. The death of Sir Tonman Mosley in 1890 would not have helped matters; Thomas Brown left the company soon afterwards, and Elton took over in probably what amounted to little more than a caretaking role. General economic and glass trade conditions were difficult, the product range likely became more utilitarian (no newspaper notices after 1890), there were no evident major changes to the factory, its managers were probably limited in their abilities, and its shareholders may have taken little interest in the business. But mere survival may be looked on as an achievement. In contrast, J.T.H. Richardson's Royal Castle Glassworks in Hatton closed its doors at the turn of the century—despite active, indeed aggressive, management by its owner-manager.

---

[150] 'Crystal Glass Manufacture at Tutbury', *Pottery Gazette and Glass Trade Review,* October 1954.
[151] *Derby Daily Telegraph,* 4 Aug 1883, 3.
[152] *Derby Daily Telegraph,* 28 Jul 1884, 2.
[153] *Lichfield Mercury,* 23 Jul 1886, 4.

Table 2. Shareholders in the Tutbury Flint Glass Company Ltd., 1882-1905.
Shares were £15 each.

				1882	1886	1894	1898	1902	1905
Allsopp	Doveridge Hall,	Hon Saml	Brewer	10	10	10	10	10	10
Arkwright	Cromford,	Jas Chas	Gentleman	15	15	15			
Arkwright	Millersley, Matlock	Fred Chas	Gentleman				15		
Thompson	Dalebrook, Burton	Francis	Brewer					15	15
Bass MP	Rangemore Hall	M.A.	Brewer	20	20	20	20	20	20
Brown	Tutbury	Thomas	Manager	5	5	5	5	5	5
Bott	Church Broughton	Richard	Gentleman	6	6	6	6		
Bott	Isthmian Club	Arthur	Gentleman					3	3
Bott	Lyme Regis	Alice Mary						3	3
Curzon	Alvaston, Derby	Wm	Gentleman	20	20	20	20	20	20
Eaton	Tutbury	Wm	Saddler	5	5	10	10	6	6
Eaton	Repton, Derbyshire	John	Wheelwright					2	2
Eaton	Stapleford, Notts	Samuel	Farmer					2	2
Elton	Tutbury	Jas	Tax Collector	5	5				
Coxon	Tutbury	Sarah Ann	Widow			5	5	5	5
Evershed	Burton-on-Trent	Sydney	Brewer	10	10	10	10	10	
Evershed	Hillside, Stapenhill	Frank	Brewer						10
Ford	Tutbury	Wm	Coal M'chant	5	5	5	5	5	5
Jackson	Tutbury	Wm Jos	Gentleman	10	10	10	10		
Jackson	Hatton	Mary	Spinster					5	5
Parrick	Tutbury	Oswald	Grocer					5	5

Table 2. Shareholders in the Tutbury Flint Glass Company Ltd., 1882-1905 (Continued).

				1882	1886	1894	1898	1902	1905
Mosley Bart	Rolleston Hall	Sir Tonman	Gentleman	85	145				
Mosley	Rolleston Hall	Sir Oswald	Baronet			49	49	49	49
Mosley	Uxbridge	Tonman	Gentleman			48	48	48	48
Mosley	London	Ernald	Gentleman			48	48	48	48
Marstons	Horninglow, Burton	John & Son	Brewers	50	20				
Turton	Wolverhampton	J.C	Gentleman			20	20	20	20
Radford	Tutbury	Edmund	Merchant	20					
Riley	Tutbury	Thos?	Glass Dealer	5	5				
Smith	Dove Cliff, Rolleston	Joseph	Gentleman	50	50				
Smith	Lichfield	Frances	Lady			50	50	50	50
Small	The Cliffe, Tutbury	Wm	Solicitor	15	15	15	15	15	15
Smith	Croydon	Alfred	Gentleman	10	10				
Smith	London	Oswald	Banker			10	10	10	
Smith	London	Eric	Banker					10	10
Storer	Tutbury	Thos	Tailor	5	5	5	5	5	5
Salt & Co	Burton-on-Trent	Thos	Brewers	10	10	10	10	10	10
Thompson	Burton-on-Trent	& Son	Brewers	15	15	15	15	15	15
Worthington	Burton-on-Trent	W.H.	Brewers	0	20	20			
Worthington	Lichfield	Albert	Gentleman	15	15	15	35	35	35
Watson	Tutbury	Thomas	Glassmaker	2	2	2	2	2	2
Knowles	Tutbury	Geo	Glass Agent	5	5	5	5	5	5
Lockett?	Liverpool	Richard R	Gentleman				30	30	30
			Total	**413**	**428**	**428**	**428**	**458**	**458**

The first signs of the Tutbury Flint Glass Company's own demise came with the inclusion of the Ludgate Street factory freehold in a 1903 auction sale by Hamptons Estate Agents of a number of Mosley family properties in the district, including East Lodge, Rolleston and several agricultural holdings. There were no buyers for the factory. But clearly the ambitions of the Mosley generations who had succeeded Sir Tonman were by now focused away from their rural Staffordshire environment and the family's financial commitment to the district was receding.

The fortunes of the factory were also receding. In December 1905, it was announced that, at Extraordinary General Meetings of the members of the company held on November 7 and 29, 1905, a special resolution was passed and confirmed: *'That the Tutbury Glass Company, Limited, be wound up voluntarily'.*[154] As of 26 February 1906, Thomas Webb & Corbett Ltd, an up-and-coming Stourbridge glassmaking firm looking to expand, reached an agreement with the liquidator of the Tutbury Glass Works Company Ltd to take over its trade and business assets. At the same time, they agreed to take on the lease of the factory from the then Baronet, Sir Oswald Mosley, and a new lease was signed on 6 July 1906, but commencing 25 March 1906, for a term of seven years at the old rent of £125 per annum. The timing of these events suggests that the purchasers had been in discussions with the Tutbury company's directors and had agreed to purchase the business before the voluntary liquidation occurred, but whether the company had actually ceased trading or not is unknown; the liquidation may have been a technical step to carry through the mechanics of the transaction.

The consideration for the purchase of the business was in the form of 1,832 new shares in Thomas Webb & Corbett Ltd. These were distributed by the liquidator to the existing shareholders of the Tutbury company, which was in due course dissolved. Some sold their new shares, some kept them; it is touching to see that the 1950s Webb Corbett shareholder register still retained a scattering of family inheritors of the original Tutbury investors who had been brought together by Tonman Mosley in 1880 to save the local factory.

In the midst of this transaction, a second large auction sale of Mosley properties was held by Sexton, Grimwade & Reek at the Tutbury Reading Room on 7 March 1906. It included 30 houses in Ludgate Street, Castle Street, and Burton Street; a blacksmith's shop and yard; 13 building sites;

---

[154] *London Gazette,* 1 Dec 1905, 8672

and the Tutbury Glass Works and Manager's House. Again, the Works did not sell. The Sale Particulars in the possession of Tutbury Museum are annotated: *'£975. Withdrawn.'*—presumably a bid that did not reach the asking price, and quite possibly a bid that came from Thomas Webb & Corbett Ltd itself. It was not until 1920 that the company did finally reach agreement to buy the freehold, at a still modest-looking price of £1,900.

Whether or not the business taken over by Thomas Webb and George Harry Corbett in 1906 was technically a going concern, it must certainly have been in a fairly moribund condition. They were particularly scathing about the unsaleability of much of the stock. But they and their successors knocked the business back into shape, and many decades of product excellence and relative prosperity followed.

Chapter 11

Conclusions

The research detailed here has provided a substantial body of new information on the history of the glass industry in Tutbury up until 1906, and the role of the Jackson family. All the available evidence substantiates Mosley's assertion that the glassworks commenced in 1810; there is no evidence of any glassworks before that time. The founder was William Jackson, whose trade up until then had been that of a grocer. William's son Henry was not the founding owner, though Henry soon took over the management of the business after his father's death in 1812. A summary timeline of key events affecting the enterprise is shown in Table 3.

These studies have also illuminated the significant part that was played by William Jackson in the religious life of Tutbury during the late eighteenth and early nineteenth centuries. By his involvement in successive attempts to establish a dissenting chapel, with their implicit criticism of the then-current practices of the Church of England, he took a principled stand that was not likely to endear him to the rural gentry; his return to the fold of the Established Church after the appointment of Cotterill as curate would not have pleased the dissenters in the village, either.

The ownership history of the Ludgate Street site within the extended Jackson family has been established. The eventual development of the glassworks was facilitated by the availability of the former meeting house and other property that William Jackson inherited from his wife's aunt, Ann Maria Congreve. Furthermore, it should not go unnoticed that Ann Moore, the notorious Fasting Woman of Tutbury, was one of William Jackson's tenants in Ludgate Street, a circumstance that led to the family's involvement in the examination and eventual exposure of Ann Moore as a fraud.

The essential facts underlying the myths about the Jackson family's connections with the United States of America have also been uncovered. Henry Jackson's two older brothers did immigrate to the United States, around 1806, and went into business as merchants, selling cut glass, china, and earthenware in Baltimore, Maryland; they were joined by William, the youngest, in 1817. They did not establish any glassmaking business in the

United States, but imported their goods, and their involvement with the trade came to an end in 1824, by which time all three of the brothers had entered the ministry of the Protestant Episcopal Church of the USA.

Table 3. Timeline of Key Events

1757	Birth of William Jackson.
1780	Marriage of William Jackson & Mary Butler.
1781-93	Births of Thomas (1781), Edward (1783), Henry (1787), and William (1793) Jackson.
1806	Thomas and Edward Jackson move to USA.
1810	William Jackson begins glassworks as cutting shop.
1812	Death of William Jackson.
	Henry Jackson takes over management.
1817	William Jackson Jr moves to USA.
1819	Marriage of Henry Jackson & Sophia Chawner.
1822	Death of Mary Butler Jackson.
1830	Death of Sophia Chawner Jackson.
1833	Marriage of Henry Jackson & Eleanor Goolden.
1836	New glassworks, including blowing shop, constructed.
1849	Death of Henry Jackson.
	Formation of the Jackson's Tutbury Glass Co.
1863	W.A. Sivewright leaves, founds Hatton glassworks.
	J.T.H. Richardson arrives.
1871	Richardson leaves, founds (Royal) Castle Flint Glass Works.
1874	Death of Eleanor Goolden Jackson.
1880	Voluntary liquidation of the Jacksons' Tutbury Glass Co.
	Formation of Mosley's Tutbury Glass Co. Ltd.
1906	Voluntary liquidation of the Tutbury Glass Co. Ltd.
	Thomas Webb & Corbett Ltd lease Tutbury glassworks.

Although not discussed in detail here, one part of the myth concerning Jackson descendants in the USA has proved to be accurate: a Jackson descendant did become a Bishop in the USA. Henry Melville Jackson (1849-1900), grandson of J. Edward Jackson and great-grandson of William Jackson, became Bishop Coadjutor of the Episcopal Diocese of Alabama, 1895-1900, though his tenure in office was cut short by his enforced resignation. Regrettably, perhaps, William Jackson's descendants did not include any Civil War Generals nor any Presidents of the USA.

The motives underlying William Jackson's venture remain uncertain, but the coincidence between the establishment of an American glass import business and an English production business cannot be ignored. The timing strongly suggests that William began his glasscutting business in response to an initiative from his USA-based sons. Lanmon has pointed out that: *'Importers of European glassware were often at the mercy of their factors' interpretations of American tastes. Few Americans established direct contact with the glass manufacturers or were lucky enough to have family connections with their European-based agents.'*[155] Clearly, a link between Edward Jackson's Baltimore store and an English glass producer would have given him a significant advantage over his competition. Furthermore, the brothers' financial interest in the prosperity of William Jackson's estate would have been a significant inducement for them to import as much of their glass as possible from Tutbury.

Unlike his brothers, Henry Jackson did not emigrate but remained in Tutbury and ran the glassworks until his death in 1849. It is possible that an export trade with his brothers in Baltimore consumed a significant part of his production during the first decade or so of the glasswork's existence, and that the East Midlands then became the focus of his sales efforts. He slowly built up the business over many years, employing more and more skills as he expanded from cutting bought-in blanks to blowing and decorating his own glass, a process which continued under his widow and children's direction from 1850 to 1880.

Although he eventually accumulated a degree of wealth and some of the trappings of a typical Victorian entrepreneur, Henry stands out in terms of his religious convictions and his intent to practice them in his business. They were likely to have been a factor in attracting workers such as William Sivewright, and consequently provided Tutbury with an important role in the development of the key union of the 1850-1880 period, the Flint Glass Makers' Friendly Society.

Sivewright's other role as the founder of the first glass factory in Hatton has finally received the recognition it deserves as a result of the research reported here. The near-simultaneous departure of Sivewright from the Ludgate Street works and the arrival of J.T.H. Richardson in Tutbury may be pure coincidence, but it is also possible that they are causally linked. Richardson's arrival seems to have revitalised the Jacksons' business. He

---

[155] Lanmon 1969, 16.

introduced new technologies and new types of wares, including pressed glass; it is ironic that the only known glassware unequivocally attributable to the Jackson era is a piece of pressed glass. He must have been the moving force behind the decision to build a second furnace and thereby modernise or expand the works, so his departure relatively soon afterwards suggests that his relationship with the Jacksons had suddenly deteriorated. Sivewright's efforts to establish a new business, although eventually unsuccessful, could also have been the catalyst that led Richardson to leave his managerial role with the Jackson family and reopen the former's works as the (Royal) Castle Flint Glass Works. Richardson's departure must have been a significant factor, along with a major decline in the economic climate, that led to the inability of the Jackson sisters to keep the business solvent, and to its closure in 1880.

The history of the Tutbury glass works in the twenty-five years after its closure by the Jacksons is a story of a valiant effort by Sir Tonman Mosley and others to keep at least a modest business alive, and to provide employment for around 50 glass makers and cutters. Little is known of the products or customers of the company during this period, though it is clear that cut glass was still being produced during Tonman Mosley's lifetime. Overall, however, the impression given by the scanty records is of a business just managing to stay alive—truly an interlude, before the arrival of Thomas Webb & Corbett Ltd and the re-emergence of the Tutbury glassworks as a significant employer and producer of high-quality lead crystal glassware, a role that was to last for yet another century.

Benjamin Bell:
A Brief Life History

Benjamin (Ben) Bell was a constant presence in the Tutbury community of glass makers in the second half of the 19th century. What is known of his working life, touching seven decades, is tabulated below as an illustration of the roller-coaster fortunes of the local industry from a worker's perspective:

1835-51: Benjamin, the younger son of Joseph and Hannah Bell, was born in 1835 in Doveridge, Derbyshire, where his father was a groom, probably for the Vicar of Doveridge. The family appears to have moved to Tutbury after 1842; Joseph died there in 1845 at the age of 50. With young children to care for, Hannah Bell soon married again. In 1847 she married Richard Bennett, a bricklayer and widower with a grown family. By 1851 the family was living in Ludgate Street, Tutbury, and Ben was working as a glassblower at Henry Jackson's glassworks. Aged 15 and the first of his family to be employed in the glass trade, it is likely that he had been working for two years or more, initially as a taker-in. His career may well have overlapped with the final years of Henry Jackson, who died in 1849.

1850s: In May 1856, Ben figured in the first full membership listing of the Flint Glass Makers' Friendly Society published in the Flint Glass Makers Magazine. His is the last name in the list of 24 members in the Tutbury District, indicating that he was the most recent entrant; it is not known if he had been formally apprenticed, but by then he was close to his 21st birthday and eligible to join the Society.

Ben married Hannah Smith, a cotton spinner, eighteen years old and carrying his child, in Tutbury in 1857. He should have been free of the shackles of any apprenticeship and earning just sufficient to support his wife and child. He signed the marriage register in a good firm hand, suggesting that he could write (and probably read) well. Between 1857 and 1881 the couple had in total four daughters and nine sons, three of whom died in infancy.

Ben appeared again on the FGMFS Membership list in 1858 and was by then probably a footmaker. The Central Committee of the Society reported in December 1859:

> *Our trade still continues in a peaceful and prosperous position, little has occurred during the past quarter out of the ordinary routine of business, except at Tutbury, where a dispute has taken place about servitors' and footmakers' wages, these being very low indeed, and after a little agitation upon the question, eleven succeeded in obtaining 2s per week advance, with proportionate overwork.*

In general, the Tutbury factory was a quiet backwater during a period that saw many difficulties in the glass trade elsewhere in the country.

1860s: Ben Bell appears to have been a model worker, making his way up the Glass Makers' rigid hierarchy in Ludgate Street, paying his Union dues on time, and never off sick. Unexpectedly, he received ten weeks unemployment pay from the FGMFS at the beginning of 1862, a rare example of a Tutbury glassmaker out of work at that time. He does not appear on the Membership roll published in 1862, perhaps because he was exempt from paying his subscription as an unemployed member. He was back on the next list in May 1864, though he received six weeks further unemployment pay at the end of that year. Significant changes were happening in the Tutbury industry at that time, with the arrival of J.T.H. Richardson to manage the Ludgate Street manufactory and the departure of William Sivewright to set up the Hatton glassworks. It is probable that Ben joined Sivewright in 1863 or 1864.

Sivewright's venture was short-lived. In June 1868 the Scropton Lane factory closed, and Ben was again on the FGMFS unemployment register, along with his Hatton colleagues. By that time, at the age of 33, he had reached the top position in the trade as a workman, which brought with it a significant increase of pay. Ben immediately found work—whether back at Ludgate Street or elsewhere in the country via the FGMFS relocation scheme is unclear—and drew unemployment pay for just one further week in August of that year.

1870s: In 1871 he was certainly working in Ludgate Street and involved in union affairs for the first time as Auditor of the Tutbury District accounts for one quarter. He and Hannah were living on Castle Street with five children. Richardson left the Jackson business in the summer of that year to set up the Castle Glass Works in Hatton, and it is likely that Ben was amongst the group of skilled workers who went with him. The next few years were a time of growth for the Hatton Glass Works, in an era of *'continued and unrivalled prosperity'* for the trade in general, with the Glass Makers' Society standing *'on a substantial foundation in the front rank of Trade Societies in the Kingdom'*. It was perhaps the prime of Ben's life, with a large family and as an established senior man amongst his work colleagues.

In 1874, Ben took on the onerous role of Secretary of the Tutbury District of the FGMFS for six months, coinciding with his first ever recorded week off work for sickness. He then held the post of Joint Auditor for the rest of the decade. Maintenance of proper financial records was a continual bugbear for 19th century trade unions, both at local and national level. The basic need was to collect and record members' regular contributions and to control benefit payments. For men who were generally untutored, this was a daunting voluntary task. Ben probably had no more formal education than his peers, though many glassblowers no doubt reached a reasonable level of numeracy just from needing to master the complex piecework wage systems under which they worked.

Around the middle of the decade, Ben's oldest son Joseph (b. 1862) followed his father in becoming a glassblower, as eventually did his brothers Ben Jr (b. 1865) and John (b. 1868). Joseph and Ben Jr were listed as glassblowers on the 1881 census, as was John in 1891. It is presumed, but not proven, that all three joined their father at the Royal Castle Glass Works, but it is possible that one or more of them worked at Ludgate Street. Joseph married, became prominent himself in the Tutbury District of the FGMFS, and then followed his trade to Stourbridge in the late 1890s. Ben Jr left the glass trade before 1886 to work in the gypsum mines at Fauld, was badly injured in an accidental explosion there in 1886, and died in 1889. John stayed in Tutbury but, as the glass trade struggled, he too switched to work at the Fauld gypsum mines. Significantly, Benjamin's three youngest sons did not follow their father's trade; prospects for steadier if lesser-skilled work than glass blowing were opening in the new industries in the area. Henry (b. 1872) and Eli (b. 1875) went to work at Fauld, and Wilfred (b. 1881) to Henri Nestlé's factory in Hatton.

1880s: Ben was Tutbury District FGMFS President from 1880 to 1882, and again in 1888/89. This was a turbulent time at the Royal Castle Glass Works. The prolonged trade depression forced J.T.H. Richardson into increasingly desperate measures to try and modify the working practices in his factory, which brought him into regular conflict with the Union.

Benjamin was the senior blower in the works and the last 20 years of his working life were spent in a context of crisis and periodic layoffs. The impact of these disputes can be traced in Ben's record of unemployment pay claims, as Richardson resorted to a pattern of temporary closures and the import of non-union labour.

Ben was out of work for 37 weeks from October 1882, when Richardson tried to introduce 'revolutionary' trade practices and brought in 'black' labour. Ben came off the unemployed register in the summer of 1883, though the deadlock continued until the end of 1885. He was probably working elsewhere in the country over this period, under the FGMFS relocation scheme—in 1884 the District paid his travel costs to London.

1890s: At the beginning of the decade, Ben was out of work for 23 weeks from December 1889, following a period in which there had been a series of disputes about pay rates, bad metal, etc. The District then paid Ben's travel costs to work in Newcastle-on-Tyne, though it is not known how long he stayed there.

The next few years were a period of continual disruptions that saw Ben and most of his colleagues laid off for a total of 47 weeks between 1892 and 1895. Then the Royal Castle Glass Works appears to have closed completely for eighteen months from May 1896, at least as far as glass blowing was concerned. Ben spent most of 1897 at St Helens and Warrington in the Lancashire glass industry, before the RCGW furnace was restarted in December.

The Hatton factory struggled back to its feet and even enjoyed a last flicker of vitality with a Royal Visit in August 1899, though for Ben this period was clouded by the death of his wife Hannah nine months earlier at the age of 60. But, in November 1899, he and his colleagues joined the FGMFS unemployment register for the last time as Richardson finally ceased glassmaking on the Scropton Lane site. He did not work again in the glass trade but continued to draw his unemployment pay until his retirement age in 1901.

Fifty years in front of a glass furnace did not seem to have overly damaged Ben's robust health. In all those years of promptly paying his fortnightly dues to the GMFS, he only called on the help of the Sick Fund for a total of twelve weeks—though he was frequently reliant, of course, on the safety net of the Unemployment Fund in his later years. Fortunately, he was able to draw his modest superannuation benefit for fifteen years after his retirement. Ben was living at 12 Castle Street in 1911 with Esther

Warin, his married daughter and her family, his FGMFS pension supplemented by the newly introduced old-age pension. He later moved to 9 Duke Street, where he died on April 19, 1917, aged 81.

Though glass blowing had declined as a source of employment for Benjamin Bell's sons, the resurgence of Webb and Corbett in Tutbury in the first half of the 20th century provided lifelong careers for several of his grandsons. Richard Bell (b. 1900) continued the family glassblowing prowess, whilst Wilfred James Bell (b. 1907), Wilfred Bell (b. 1909), and Douglas Bell (b. 1920) became skilled glass cutters, overlapping with the final Tutbury Crystal Glass era of the village industry. Dick Bell and the two Wilfs were old enough to have known Ben in his last years. Remarkably therefore, between grandfather and grandsons, the Bell family bridged the entire ownership history of the Ludgate Street factory, from Henry Jackson in the 1840s to the co-operative venture in the 1980s.

Sources

Alexander, S D 1887. *The Presbytery of New York, 1738 to 1888.* New York, NY: Anson D.F. Randolph & Co.

Anon., 1809. *An account of the extraordinary abstinence of Ann Moor of Tutbury.* Uttoxeter: R. Richards.

Anon., 1813. *A full exposure of Ann Moore, the pretended fasting woman of Tutbury.* London: Robert Baldwin.

Anon., [1843]. *An historical description of Tutbury Castle and Priory, with some account of the town and neighbourhood.* Tutbury: H. Wayte.

B.B., [Brook, Benjamin] 1820. Memoir of the late Mr. Francis Greasley, of Tutbury, Staffordshire. *The Evangelical Magazine and Missionary Chronicle* **28**, 463-66.

Cummins, G D 1856. *A Sketch of the life of the Rev. William M. Jackson, Late Rector of St. Paul's Church, Norfolk, VA.* New York, NY: Protestant Episcopal Society for the Promotion of Evangelical Knowledge.

Donaldson, B 1960. *The registration of dissenting chapels and meeting houses in Staffordshire, 1689-1852.* Collections for a History of Staffordshire, 4th Series, Vol. III.

Ellis, J 2002. *Glassmakers of Stourbridge and Dudley, 1612-2002: A biographical history of a once great industry.* Harrogate: Jason Ellis.

Hajdamach, C R 1991. *British glass 1800-1914.* Woodbridge: Antique Collectors' Club.

Hewitson, C 2005. *Tutbury Crystal Glassworks, Burton Street, Tutbury, Staffordshire: An historic building recording and assessment.* Birmingham: Birmingham Archeology.

Jackson, M A 1861. *Memoirs of the Rev. William Jackson, first Rector of St. Paul's Church, Louisville.* New York, NY: Protestant Episcopal Society for the Promotion of Evangelical Knowledge.

Jackson, W M 1847. *Remains of the Rev. William Jackson, late Rector of St. Paul's Church, Louisville, KY.* New York, NY: Stanford & Swords.

Lanmon, D P 1969. The Baltimore glass trade, 1780 to 1820. *Winterthur Portfolio* **5**, 15-48.

Matsumura, T 1976. *The flint glass makers in the classic age of the labour aristocracy, 1850-1880, with special reference to Stourbridge.* Ph.D. Thesis, University of Warwick.

Matsumura, T 1983. *The labour aristocracy revisited. The Victorian flint glass makers 1850-80.* Manchester: Manchester University Press.

Marx, K 1887. *Capital: A critical analysis of capitalist production.* 1st English Ed. London: Swan Sonnenschein, Lowrey & Co.

Matthews, A G 1924. *The Congregational churches of Staffordshire: with some account of the Puritans, Presbyterians, Baptists and Quakers in the county during the 17th century.* London: Congregational Union of England and Wales.

Mosley, O 1832. *History of the castle, priory, and town of Tutbury in the county of Stafford.* London: Longman & Co.

Richmond, L 1813. *A statement of facts relative to the supposed abstinence of Ann Moore, of Tutbury, Staffordshire.* Burton-on-Trent: J. Croft.

Scharf, J T 1881. *History of Baltimore city and county from the earliest period to the present day.* Philadelphia, PA: Louis H. Everts.

Tacchella, B 1902. *The Derby School register.* London: Bemrose & Sons Ltd.

Tringham, N J ed. 2007. *The Victoria history of the county of Stafford X, Tutbury and Needwood Forest.* Woodbridge: Boydell and Brewer.

Underhill, C H 1949. *History of Tutbury and Rolleston.* Burton upon Trent: Tresises.

White, W 1834, 1851. *History, gazetteer and directory of Staffordshire.* Sheffield: W. White.

Acknowledgments

We are most grateful to the following:

Robert and Jeanne Minchin, volunteers at Tutbury Museum, for the untold hours they have devoted to transcribing the parochial and census records for Tutbury and making them available in digital format. Those digital records have been invaluable in our research. We also thank Robert for many helpful discussions.

Tutbury Museum, for granting permission to reproduce the images shown in Figs 10, 11, 13, 20, 22, 23, 27, 28, 30 and the Frontispiece.

The Vicar and Churchwardens of St. Mary's Priory Church, Tutbury, for permission to reproduce the photograph of the glassworks cone shown in Fig. 18.

The Special Collections Department (Debra Elfenbein, Librarian) of the Enoch Pratt Free Library, Baltimore, MD, USA, for permission to reproduce the images from the Cator Collection of Baltimore Views shown in Figs 8 and 9.

Ken Burns of the Rakow Research Library, Corning Museum of Glass, Corning, NY, USA, for organising our access to a digital version of the Maryland Historical Society's microfilm of the Matthew Smith letterbooks.

Ian Dury of the Webb Corbett Visitor Centre (now the Glasshouse Heritage Centre), Stourbridge, for the image of the FGMFS membership certificate shown in Fig. 29.

Adam Fileman of Fileman Antiques, Steyning, West Sussex, for providing the images of Regency glass used on the front and rear covers.

We also thank our wives, Janie and Penny, for their forbearance and understanding over the years this project has lasted.

About the Authors

Philip Bell and Chris Tipper are both natives of Tutbury and sons of life-long Tutbury glass cutters. Many of their ancestors and extended families spent their working lives in the local glassmaking industry. Philip is a retired research scientist with a PhD in biochemistry. His career encompassed both academic research in the life sciences and senior research management in the global pharmaceutical industry. He now lives in the United States. Chris is a retired Chartered Accountant and Finance Director, and a Trustee of Tutbury Museum